PRAISE FOR THE AUTHOR

'I've known Rakhee for the last ten years. I've seen her convert an idea into a successful business and know that she is passionate about every recipe that she teaches. I have great respect for her work and believe that if you're passionate about what you do, you will definitely succeed. It's always difficult to make people change their food habits (which is mostly born out of laziness or habit). It's a matter of teaching people to make good choices six days a week and allowing them to cheat on the seventh day. I'm eagerly awaiting the release of this book to own a copy and keep a stack of it in my gym for my clients.'

—Yasmin Karachiwala

'I had never entered the kitchen before I met Rakhee but she transformed me into a master chef. I wasn't ever interested in cooking until recently, when I felt the need to know my basics. With my growing interest, I approached Rakhee and that was the best decision I ever made. As soon as I entered Palate Culinary Studio at Santacruz, I was enchanted with the vibe and the ambience of the place. Rakhee personally helped me learn everything, from the basics to desserts, and I kept going back to her for over a year. She is the best person to learn cooking from. With over a hundred classes and new inventions every month, she is a real cooking star. I'm so thankful to my friends who referred her name to me. Learning with her is a delightful and fun experience and anyone who has a passion for cooking and wants to learn more should definitely go to her.'

—Sunita Menon

'Rakhee is a very passionate chef. When I met her, I was at a stage where I wanted to please my family with simple, exotic dishes. She made learning so uncomplicated that today I can cook a range of wonderful cuisines and Shaan and the kids think I am a master chef! My knowledge about the culinary world and confidence in the kitchen also helped me entertain friends with different dishes. Learning at her beautifully done up studio is like working in a warm kitchen which has only one word, one feel to it—food. I believe good food is like medicine to the soul. Nowadays when we are entertaining, my dining table boasts of a beautifully roasted, juicy leg of madras chicken with some grilled vegetables and a side of focaccia bread, among other things.'

—Radhika Mukherji

PICKY EATERS

And Other Meal-Time Battles

Rakhee Vaswani

EBURY PRESS
An imprint of Penguin Random House

EBURY PRESS

USA | Canada | UK | Ireland | Australia
New Zealand | India | South Africa | China | Singapore

Ebury Press is part of the Penguin Random House group of companies.
whose addresses can be found at global.penguinrandomhouse.com

Published by Penguin Random House India Pvt. Ltd
4th Floor, Capital Tower 1, MG Road,
Gurugram 122 002, Haryana, India

Penguin Random House India

First published by Random House India 2015

Illustrations by Ritesh Waingankar

10 9 8 7 6 5 4 3 2

ISBN 9788184006032

The views and opinions expressed in this book are the author's own and the facts are as reported by her which have been verified to the extent possible, and the publishers are not in any way liable for the same.

Typeset in Sabon by Manipal Digital Systems, Manipal
Printed at Repro India Limited

www.penguin.co.in

FSC www.fsc.org MIX Paper from responsible sources FSC® C047271

This is a legitimate digitally printed version of the book and therefore might not have certain extra finishing on the cover.

This is for you, and only you . . .

Contents

PART TWO

Recipes

Foreword

I OWE ALL my cooking, or the experience of it, to Rakhee. She is the most humble, patient and wonderful teacher I have come across (obviously the only one!). She makes teaching and learning a very pleasurable experience. I have had the great fortune of attending many classes at Palate Culinary Studio with Rakhee but by far the best experience I have had was at the 'Hands-On Sushi Making Class'. People think making sushi is tedious and difficult but her hands-on class, where I learnt how to roll and create amazing sushi was the best experience I have had.

My son, Arhaan, loved experimenting with food and tried stuff like sushi and caviar at a very young age. I guess he imbibed all his eating habits from me. As he was always very adventurous, my whole process of learning began when he started coming back from school, rattling off how other mothers would make yummy food. So I took up the challenge and entered the kitchen. Thankfully, he never indulged in junk food and always preferred home food. It's not that he does not like going out, but he prefers home-cooked meals. Hence I didn't have to worry on that front.

Arhaan hates tomatoes, particularly if he sees the seeds and skin, so I have to camouflage it. I remember sharing this with Rakhee and doing a Conti Meal class with her—which has a beautiful, wholesome menu to entice your family—and it really made me feel like a master chef. She taught me how to make paprika sauce by camouflaging the tomato and now Arhaan simply loves it with grilled chicken.

Since he hated tomatoes, I had to cheat him for his own good. If he sees it in his dal or subzi he would never touch it, hence pureeing or sieving was always a better way out. Arhaan enjoys his veggies—I totally attribute this to our upbringing—so I have introduced fish, rice and vegetables in his daily diet as we have grown up eating this and he is absolutely okay with it. I always take him with me when I go grocery-shopping. He loves it the most. In fact, he has also accompanied me to workshops at Palate Culinary Studio.

Basically my good food habits have totally rubbed off on him. While I was growing up, my mom was very particular about our lunch and dinner, so yes, following good eating habits is a must.

Family meals are very essential too as husbands are at work and kids are at school all day long. So dinner becomes the most important meal of the family. It's important to share one meal and have healthy discussions around it.

Arhaan always likes to explore different food preparations online and experiment with his friends' lunch boxes. I remember once he came home and asked me to make something with Soba Noodles and chicken and gave a lot of descriptions. . . I just picked up the phone and asked Rakhee for help. This is the best part about her—cooking is such a passion that give her a brief, or just few keywords, and a recipe flows out of her. As I was learning something new every day, Arhaan's complaining eventually stopped and now he thinks I am the best chef in the world.

Malaika Arora Khan

Introduction

WHEN I LOOK at myself in the mirror, I see an empowered woman, respected and confident in her own skin. However, my journey to where I stand now hasn't been an easy one. I come from an orthodox Sindhi family where women are mostly kept in the confines of the home, so working was never an option for me. At one point, I longed to become a choreographer or try my luck at acting, but I could never really pursue my dreams. Luckily, since learning how to cook was an essential part of growing up, I would spend most of my free time as a kid in my aunt's kitchen, learning her secrets to a yummy curry or even something as simple as dal and rice. *I would love helping out and picking up tips from my aunts.*

My culinary journey began with simple cooking classes at home and I slowly moved on to experimenting and learning newer styles. I started my own cooking classes at home with a partner and one day—I was at my peak at the time—gave it all up to be a hands-on mother. It was a small sacrifice but my children pushed me back in the same direction years later to follow my dream.

From enrolling for a bakery course at Sophia's, I moved on to attain my Cordon Bleu certificate in London.

By now I had already set up Palate Culinary Studio in Mumbai, a first-of-its-kind international cooking school with a state-of-the-art kitchen—a space where one could learn and cook like a master chef. I wanted to share with the world the wonders of cooking, to intrigue and inspire little kids, to provide teenagers with a way to pass their time, to help out newly-wed wives in desperate need of impressing their families, to provide home cooks, like I earlier was, a platform to expand their horizons and learn simple yet complex dishes they never dreamed of cooking in their lives. I set out on my endeavour simply to accomplish what I thought was second nature to me. I used to teach in a school in the early years of my life and cooking is my passion, so the idea of a cooking school came to me like a brainwave.

I am very proud of the fact that at the age of thirty-eight, when most people hang up their work coats, I made a successful career out of my passion. I hope to inspire many others with my own example.

Food and its role in my life

Food has been a constant in all our lives mainly because we need it in order to survive. However, when I think of food, it's not just a meal to fill a stomach, it is so much bigger than that. To me, food is the aroma of spices being tossed over the fire causing a smoky haze before the eyes; it's the burst of flavour on my tongue as I taste the concoction on my spoon before serving it up; it's the smiles on the faces of my friends and family as they devour the dish I've prepared. Food to me is not simply 'food'. I am emotionally, spiritually and physically attached to it. For those of you who think I'm rambling, don't worry, this is still a cookbook and not a romance novel. ☺

My food journey has been really long. I've travelled around the globe in search of perfect food and have tasted cuisines from the world over. My kids sampled a sea urchin and octopus pizza at an early age while on a cruise. They've also tasted frog legs, escargot and many other seemingly weird dishes because my adventurous husband, Mahesh, believes that it's always better to try something new for the sake of the experience than to never know what it tastes like.

The way I look at it, food *can* make you happy. It has been present in all things since the beginning of time. What do you offer someone when they come home? Or when it's someone's birthday? You eat, because a meal is always fulfilling and it's nice to enjoy a good meal after a bad day at work, or school for that matter. Whether it's a nice curry or a sandwich, or even munchies—food always makes you feel better. Haven't you had that day when you feel utterly frustrated but as soon as you walk into your home, or pass by the *Khao Galli* in your area, the aroma consumes you in a passionate embrace like no other? It seduces your senses and you know everything will get better as long as your stomach is happy.

It's easy to be inspired and create great food

I love to eat and hence I love cooking. But to be inspired and motivated to try and create something new that satiates the palate comes when someone close to your heart guides you, criticizes you, praises you and gives you honest feedback in every way so you grow and become better. It is this exactly this—coming from one source—that has kept me going for so long. The biggest support system in my life, my husband, provided me with the tools and the motivation required to reach where I am right now. Being a Gemini and a food connoisseur, he has always made me reach out and learn something new every day, which is my biggest strength today.

It's really important to me that people can cook and recreate my recipes. My culinary school today boasts of more than 100 one-day workshops in cuisines from all over the world! Mahesh would criticize my new trials before a launch in the class or any new recipe without even blinking an eye. His reasoning was that if the food hasn't turned out great, I need to tell you. He always rates me on a scale of one to ten which helps me analyse because you can't always get the perfect balance; some recipes need a lot of research and development.

The other two people in my life who have been more than supportive all through my journey are my daughter and son. Both are huge foodies and while my daughter's favourite dish is sushi, my son loves his smoked salmon. Our family is very vocal about the passion we have for food—we tend to always know the best restaurants to which to take our visiting friends and family. Right now if you ask my son the best joint in town for a particular dish, he will tell you in an instant. My children, who are now eighteen and sixteen, have an amazing palate and know their food from right to wrong, from flavours to appeal. This is because while they were growing up,

Mahesh and I would always expose them to different kinds of food and we would never force anything down their throat. So if they didn't like something, we would let it be.

Eating out is one of the greatest pleasures of life but I have made it a mission to create restaurant food at home for fussy eaters. The key to making your children try new things, I realized, is to let them do it at their own pace.

Getting back into the industry wasn't so hard on my children as I had imagined it would be because they were both growing into their teens and wanted me out of their hair. All I can say is I love them for it, as now I am on a path to learn as much as I can with them as my judges, always ready with their expert opinion.

My kitchen, my safe haven

My kitchen is my paradise. I could have a high fever, but I would still wake up and go to work. At home, I am relaxed when I cook and therefore it's in those moments that I brainstorm and try to think of new ideas and explore new types of cuisine. I love finding quick methods of cooking and taking shortcuts.

I like to keep my kitchen workstation absolutely clean because then it feels like it's inviting me to create. I love the sizzle of butter in the pan, the marriage of butter and garlic—it's a match made in heaven— the smell of freshly baked bread. It's so therapeutic to knead the dough and shape it into beautiful creations, ready to be massacred by some hungry beasts. I love a busy kitchen with everyone running in all directions. It gives me a feeling of pride and gratitude towards God who blessed me with this wonderful gift.

There's more to a kitchen than what meets the eye. It is not only a room in which I cook and create but also a place where I spend the greater part of my day. It's almost as if I live there. It feels like I can talk and listen more clearly while chopping vegetables, stirring a soup or frying chicken. I feel my senses sharpen in the kitchen, as though I were a majestic hawk focusing on my prey. The kitchen is like a newborn baby to me and I love buying new toys for it. I love dressing it up with souvenirs of my visits to different food havens or markets. I kind of feel it smiles at me in gratitude. You must think I'm being silly but this little connection is what keeps me coming back for more.

I started cooking at home for my family when I was merely thirteen and have been on a learning journey since then. I've always loved eating good food and since I teach people, I have tried to do something new and exciting with each recipe the second time around. Anyway, enough about me, so let's get cooking!

Why This Book?

THIS RECIPE BOOK aims to provide a platform to mothers like me who have (or in my case, had) picky eaters at home. The importance of good childhood nutrition has never been more topical. The role parents play in establishing the foundation of the right nutrition for a child cannot be overstated. A child needs to be taught right from wrong—not only in the way they talk or act but also in what they eat. Parents are constantly reminded of the need to offer their children healthy, home-cooked meals and the importance of cutting down on fatty and unhealthy food. However, with the crazy, fast-paced lifestyle we parents lead, there is barely any time for the family. The constant juggling act between work, social life and domesticity makes regular home cooking—to ensure a nutritious diet for every family member—an impossible ideal. It is a truth universally acknowledged that quick, easily prepared food often simply means very unhealthy meals. After all, isn't it so much easier to make pasta than dal, rice and subzi? And there is the taste factor as well, isn't there, fellow parents? Haven't you had days when you've packed a proper, healthy meal for your kid's tiffin only to have it come back untouched? The subtle rejection stings and we end up sending them off with a salami sandwich the next day. Through my book, I want to guide both mothers and kids alike. My primary objective in writing this book is to make everyone realize that when it comes to food, the Holy Trinity is possible. It can be healthy, tasty and easy to make. I hope you have as much fun reading this book as I had writing it.

Simplicity is the key to my book. All the recipes I use might have overwhelmingly complex names but these have been abridged to cater to the needs of my main customers, my fellow mothers. I adopted a realistic approach to the demands of modern-day parenting, carefully taking into account the time crunches we have to work with. Yet, my recipes provide the nutrition essential for your kids. This family cookbook includes recipes that traverse a wide range of culinary experiences, from the absolute basic to party-themed creations. I also include a bunch of parent–kid cook-along recipes, consequently making cooking an enjoyable, bonding experience for all. It makes for a good mix of nutritional, healthy, wholesome and fun recipes you can use for any occasion.

The essence of my recipes can be captured in one word—FRESH. Nothing, absolutely nothing, is better than dewy-fresh ingredients. *My aunt always taught me that a great cook is one who spends more time sourcing the right ingredients than spending hours in the kitchen.* On Sundays we'd have big family lunches where the food was always simple yet full of flavour.

I have endless food memories from my childhood, but the most vivid are the Sundays I spent watching my mom make her special lamb chops with five simple ingredients which we relished at the lunch table. Ultimately, it's the people you eat with and the connection you make with flavours that form a big part of your life.

My most ardent wish is to have a garden of my own—a nigh impossible dream in our corporate-jungle existence. In this book you will not see any tinned or canned food being used and all the recipes begin from scratch. I have learnt from experience that if we portion our meals and only eat enough to replenish ourselves every two hours, we can feed our beloved picky eaters all the stuff they like and yet not worry about the calories. Bon appétit!

Kitchen Basics

HERE I PRESENT some basics of cooking to turn you into a *MasterChef* mummy or, in some post-feminist cases, daddy. Once you are through, packing a lunch should take very little time and as few dirty dishes as possible. If you follow a few key rules and plan your steps in advance, you will spend only a brief period in the kitchen every morning. But before that, I would like to give you an extensive overview of the must-haves in every kitchen.

UTENSILS

I think you can never have enough utensils but you should know which ones are essential to any type of cooking. It is also important to know the proper way to deal with them and keep them in good condition to ensure their longevity.

Pans

A non-stick pan in two or three different sizes is an absolute essential in any modern kitchen. I am particularly fond of a small 5-inch one for my eggs—it's a fun way to make your own individual frittata or mini pancakes. Apart from that, you should have the regular 24-inch pans which can handle all your sautéing and stir-frying. Since these are non-stick, it's super easy to pan-fry all your cutlets and snacks in minimum oil and still maintain their shape and taste.

Wok

A 20-inch-diameter wok is a must-have in your kitchen for all the fancy wok fries and stir-fries, an amazing fried rice, or some hot Mongolian stir-fry. These are available at all station roads for a mere Rs 350 to Rs 400 and you must season them as they are iron-based. They both heat up and cool down very fast.

Seasoning of the wok: Place all your vegetable peels in the wok instead of throwing them away. Fill it with water up to the brim and let it simmer on the flame for 25 minutes. This gets rid of all the carbon deposits which could otherwise settle in your system. Throw the water and the peels, wash thoroughly and dry your wok with a napkin. Rub a layer of oil on it to avoid rusting. Repeat this process once more and your wok is ready to use.

My personal tip: If you stay near the sea, always rub some oil on your wok to avoid rusting.

Also, if you are using your wok after a few months, please repeat the seasoning process before cooking in it.

Bakeware

For me, the process of baking is an utter delight—from the mixing of the batter to when the aroma starts wafting out of the kitchen and into the rest of the house once the oven door is opened. Nothing can match up to this pure, visceral pleasure. I have a range of baking tins for my cupcakes, cakes and loaves, Bundt pans and ring moulds.

Here is a list of essential bakeware:

- Cupcake moulds: mini and regular size
- Ring moulds: one of each size—5-inch and 6-inch (great for all cheesecakes or mousse cakes; I even like to make my brownies in these as they give them a better shape)
- Loaf tins: two of 7x3 inches (for all your teatime cakes and breads)
- Round cake tins: 6-inch, 7-inch, 9-inch (for sponge cakes)
- Square cake tins: 6-inch, 9-inch and 10-inch (for sponge cakes, brownies and some light bites or muesli)
- Palette knife
- Spatula
- Whisk

GADGETS

I am technologically challenged but still like to have all the fancy equipment in my kitchen that is easy to use.

Let's start with the basics.

Hand blender

This gadget comes with two rods. It helps with all your blending and baking needs, from creaming butter and sugar for your cupcakes to whipping cream or even beating egg whites stiff for a meringue.

You get these in all stores, and for as low as Rs 1200.

Convection oven

This is a must-have if you're into baking, grilling, roasting, or if you want to entice your picky eater with pizza and fancy treats. A convection oven comes with a coil above and below and with a fan option which distributes the heat evenly. If you opt for the fan, you can get even baking done and don't have to turn your cookies around. There are many brands to choose from in the market, like Morphy Richards, Bajaj and so on. I prefer KitchenAid because it is reasonably priced and therefore perfect for the home kitchen. If you fancy a more professional approach, I suggest a Whirlpool which looks pretty in the kitchen as a built-in.

Food processor

This is a multipurpose machine which can do all your chopping, blending and milling in the kitchen. Whether or not to buy it depends on the scale and complexity of your cooking. Buy it if you expect to cook big, intricate meals, even semi-regularly and have the requisite kitchen space. If not, I recommend that you stick to a blender.

Mixer-grinder

This machine ends up doing all the work in our kitchens and is perfect for Indian homes. I've grown up using a Bajaj.

Sandwich griller

I like to grill sandwiches and make my fancy panini and even quesadillas in this. It is an ideal gadget for your picky eater's use as well.

Apart from the ones mentioned above, you can have a few more fancy gadgets on your shelves, like a smoothie maker, juicer, pasta maker, planetary mixer (if you are a master baker) and even an ice-cream maker. But these are all extra luxury items you can do without.

A list of additional must-haves in the kitchen cupboard:

- Scissors: in two sizes

- A good set of knives: an 8-inch chef's knife, paring, carving, serrated knife
- Gloves or oven mittens
- Chopping board
- Ladles
- Strainers/colander
- Micro plane
- Grater (preferably a box grater)
- Potato masher
- Mortar and pestle (the stone one has an appealing rusticity about it)

COOKING

First, I am going to give you a couple of simple recipes to ease yourself in the kitchen. These are the most basic of recipes but following them correctly can still be a task. Why is it that when you make fried rice, it sometimes becomes clumpy and mushy? I get this and many other similar questions from my students, hence the following tips:

Vegetable and chicken stock

You are probably wondering why I am giving you the recipe for stock. The thing is that most people use Maggi chicken or vegetable stock cubes in order to season their food. However, they don't realize how unhealthy it is and how many preservatives it contains. Therefore, I'm going to show you how to make your own stock.

Vegetable stock

For a simple vegetable stock, all you need is a medium-sized carrot, a couple of beans, some mushroom stems, two stalks of celery, one onion, one clove of garlic, a couple of peppercorns, one bay leaf and, of course, water. Put all the vegetables in a pot with 750 ml of water and bring it to a boil. Reduce the heat and let it simmer for 30 minutes until the water reduces to 600 ml. Strain and use as required.

Chicken Stock

Take 100 grams of chicken bones and add to 750 ml of water. Bring it to a boil. Reduce the heat and let it simmer for 30 minutes until it reduces to 600 ml. Strain and use as required.

Red chilli paste

This is a really simple yet essential ingredient to keep in your kitchen. What you need is 15–20 Kashmiri red chillies and just 1 tbsp of oil. Slit the chillies and remove the seeds. Soak them for 15–20 minutes in warm water. Grind to a smooth paste, adding a little oil gradually.

Chef's Tip

Always rub a little oil on your hands before cutting or chopping the red chilli. The paste can be bottled and refrigerated for up to a week.

Blanching of vegetables

Broccoli, corn, carrot, baby corn, beans

Take a lot of water in a vessel and add salt to it. Bring it to a boil. Add every vegetable separately and boil for 3–4 minutes. Take them out and soak them in cold water to maintain their colour, texture and crunchiness, and to prevent overcooking.

Before adding the next vegetable, bring the water back to boiling point and replenish it with salt. Always start with the whites and then proceed to the greens. This water can also be used as stock.

Rice

To boil rice

Boil rice with lots of salty water, for e.g. 1 cup rice should be boiled with 4 cups of water and a lot of salt.

Cook the rice till it's about 95 per cent done and then strain it in a colander. Rinse and wash out the starch with fresh cold water, letting it drain for an hour. Transfer to another dish and refrigerate. (Do this in advance for fried rice and stir-fry.)

Fried rice

Refrigerated rice that is a day old is best for fried rice. Take your vegetables and sauté them in an oil of your choice. Cook for 3–4 minutes. Take care that vegetables are not overdone; they should be crisp. Add salt and pepper to taste. Then add the cooked rice and mix well. Now add soya sauce to it. The proportion should be half a tablespoon of soya sauce for one cup of rice. This Chinese fried rice should be cooked for 2–3 minutes and served hot.

Pulao rice
The saltiness should be just right and the rice should not be mushy.

Ratio of rice to water for pulao varies. For example, 1 cup of rice needs 2 cups of water. The water should be salty.

Chef's Tip

Use stock for nutrition and to add an extra punch.

Sautéing

Sautéing (from the French sauté, literally meaning 'jumped, bounced' with reference to tossing while cooking) is a method of cooking that involves using a small amount of oil or fat in a shallow pan over relatively high heat. Ingredients are usually cut into pieces or thinly sliced to facilitate fast cooking. The primary mode of heat transfer during sautéing is conduction between the pan and the food being cooked. Food that is sautéed is browned while preserving its texture, moisture and flavour. If meat, chicken or fish is sautéed, the residue in the pan can be deglazed to make a sauce.

Poaching

In the culinary arts, the word 'poach' refers to cooking something in its liquid state at a temperature ranging from 140°F to 180°F. Poaching is typically reserved for cooking very delicate items like eggs and fish. Other protein-based food items like chicken are sometimes prepared by poaching, and some vegetables can be poached too.

The advantage of poaching as a cooking technique is that the poached items will turn out moist and tender which is certainly desirable in the case of fish which dries out very easily if prepared using other cooking methods. And because poaching involves keeping the cooking liquid at a constant temperature—a fairly low one at that—it makes it less likely that the items will be overcooked. At least, it would take a lot longer to overcook something.

The liquid used for poaching is usually stock or water, with seasoning and aromatic vegetables. The water in which fish or seafood is poached can further act as a stock to make sauces.

Hard boiling eggs

Put eggs in a small saucepan and add cold water to cover. Place over high heat and once the water comes to a boil, reduce the heat and let the eggs simmer for 12 minutes. Rinse with cold water once done and carefully peel the shell off each egg.

PART ONE

1

Is Your Child a Picky Eater?

Here is a short questionnaire for parents to assess whether their child is a picky eater or not.

1. Does your child make a face at whatever is served at mealtime?

   YES NO

2. Does your child have an aversion to everything green?

   YES NO

3. Do you have a difficult time convincing your child to eat any vegetable besides potato?

   YES NO

4. Is the response to junk food always a big, excited YES and home food a melancholic NO?

   YES NO

5. If introduced to a new food item, a disgusted expression automatically appears on your child's face or a huge fuss is created.

   YES NO

6. Is non-vegetarian food preferred over vegetarian?

   YES NO

7. Does your child always eat a lot of snack food items, like chips and instant noodles, and then say they aren't hungry at mealtimes?

   YES NO

8. Is there always space in their stomach for dessert, whereas the plate of food is left untouched?

   YES NO

9. Does your child watch TV while eating and play with their food?

   YES NO

10. Do most of your fights begin with 'Finish your food', 'Why aren't you eating?' or 'If you don't eat what is on your plate, no ice cream for you'?

    YES NO

Once you have answered the questions above, it is time to find out if you need to worry. The answer is simple. If your answer was 'yes' for more than four questions, then your child is a picky eater. But since this phenomenon is very common, you don't need to worry. Read on to find out how to remedy the situation.

It's so easy to feel frustrated when you have spent time making food and your picky eater refuses to eat. This is a common situation in many homes as a result of which mothers feel helpless. They often wonder if it is only their child who is behaving like that. From my experience with my daughter who went through a phase where she would not touch any food item that threatened nutrition, I can tell you that I empathize. Over the years I have seen lots of children go through at least one lengthy phase of picky eating. While it can be frustrating when a child rejects the food we give them, their eating habits are impacted in a major way by how we react to the situation. Healthy eating habits and tastes can be instilled in them with a little thought and some smart moves in the kitchen.

One of the most important things to do is to try and make mealtimes a fun, positive experience. Hide any frustration you might have and shower your child with praise when he/she eats well or tries something new. This may mean that you have to ignore some of their bad behaviour.

Picky eating is common in young children, with up to a third of children around two years of age going through this stage. Picky eaters generally refuse to eat, exhibit a lack of interest in food and eat slowly and, in some cases, have a reduced appetite.

This, however, is usually a phase that children outgrow once past their formative years. Having said that, this phase can still be stressful for parents, particularly at mealtimes or while packing their lunches. Parents, naturally, worry that their child is missing out on adequate nutrition which makes them concerned about the general health of their picky eater, which in turn may start affecting their performance in school and their overall development, physically and mentally. However, it's more important to ensure that they have acquired adequate nutrition over a prolonged period of time. Therefore instead of worrying about what they ate over a week, one should keep a check on what kind of nutrition their child acquires in a day or through a particular meal. Basically, look at the larger picture. Picky eating is like a disease caused by a number of factors. Once you figure out the symptoms, finding the cure will be easier.

Your child—especially if he/she is a toddler—may be experiencing a growing sense of independence. Refusing food can be a way of asserting themselves.

A big or sudden change in a child's life and environment—moving houses, starting a playgroup or the birth of a sibling, for instance—can also lead to difficult behaviour like refusal of food. It's a way of seeking attention.

A recent survey of caregivers showed that people often made only three to five attempts when introducing a new food to a child. However, research suggests that young children need more than ten exposures to a new food before they accept it. Perseverance is thc key!

To help tackle that hurdle, it is better to have a weekly plan in order to fulfil all necessary nutritional requirements.

Here are some common questions going through parents' minds:

Q. How common is picky eating among children?

A. Dear readers, the fact of the matter is that it's not just common but absolutely normal. Picky eating is a problem that binds us in a community since it is faced by most parents, regardless of the age of their child.

Q. Will my child grow out of being a picky eater?

A. This is the issue parents stress about the most. Picky eating is a problem but if it becomes a lifestyle, it's a catastrophe. However, this is not something to lose sleep over. Like I said, it's a phase and it goes away as surely as day follows night. It could be the influence of your child's peers or simply boredom that makes your child finally stop fussing and start eating properly. For pre-teens, moms needn't worry because by the time children reach their teenage years it's in their nature to be bolder in their choices, not only in dating and music, but even in food.

Q. What important food should my child include in his/her diet?

A. All food groups are important but most of us forget to provide a certain food group in the amount that is required. These are called superfoods. They are rich in antioxidants and provide your children with vitamins and minerals, even when they are consumed in small amounts. (Read Chapter 4 for more information on superfoods.)

Q. How can I help my child get through their picky eating phase?

A. *Kyunki saas bhi kabhi bahu thi.* The same way all parents were kids once, right? Just take a stroll down memory lane and go back to the time when you were a picky eater yourself. Wasn't it the most annoying thing in the whole wide world to be forced into eating things you didn't want to? Eventually, your parents stopped nagging and you started liking even your veggies. So let your children be and avoid forcing them into eating things they don't like.

Q. Should I speak to my doctor about my child's picky eating?

A. This is like asking to go to a surgeon for a paper cut. Why would you go to a doctor for such a simple issue? In fact, it isn't even an issue. Like I said before, this is completely normal.

Q. What can I do to avoid feeling stressed or frustrated when my child is being picky with food?

A. In the later chapters I'll tell you in complete detail what I used to do when my kids would make a fuss. If you get stressed, they might reject all food. As a last resort, remove yourself from the room to cool off and regain equilibrium.

Below is an example of a parent and her turmoil during this phase. It might throw some light on the matter for you:

Sonya is a friend of mine who, like many Indian women, lives in a joint family. It can be very difficult to plan separate meals or fancy food for your fussy eater in such a situation since meals have to be made keeping everyone in mind. Sometimes it can get boring and monotonous. Her younger child is an athlete and so she has to follow some diet restrictions and, at times, load him up on carbs and proteins. Very often, mothers feel that pulses do not have enough protein to meet the daily requirements but it is not possible to prepare chicken or fish every day. Being a mother of a fussy eater often teaches you how to deal with such situations. Sonya has found a smart way around the problem by including dates and figs in her son's diet, giving him date and banana milkshakes after his swimming practice. She also ensures that he gets his fish and chicken two to three times a week outside the house and twice at home, which is a nice balance that he needs in his growing years.

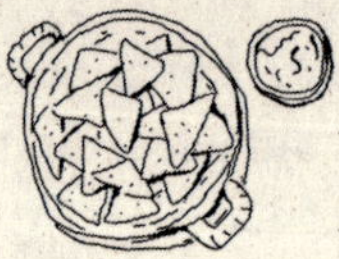

2

Establishing a Healthy Food Culture in the House

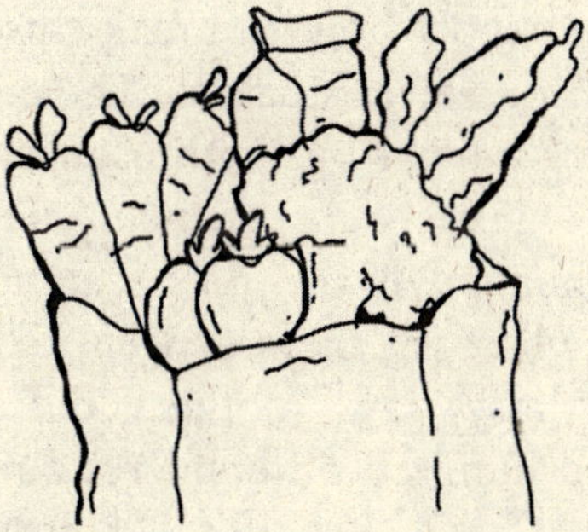

I KNOW THIS sounds ominously like the beginning of a really long and boring lecture about kitchen management but trust me parents, you will not regret it. I know how ugly things can get when the food that is being served at the table is not appealing to the eyes. My own kids have thrown multiple fits, so I can legitimately claim that I've been there, done that. All you can do then is order takeout—which breaks your heart, doesn't it? I can completely relate to the way you feel. You are angry, frustrated and, most of all, disappointed that the food you slaved over in the kitchen after working the whole day has been left untouched. Homemakers have it worse since this rejection comes on top of a day already filled with endless hard labour. I used to be one for most of my life so I know the mechanics. No worries, ladies and gentlemen, your sorrows in this department are about to end.

You need to know how to break this vicious cycle that we all find ourselves stuck in. The demands of the stomach need to be met but with a different approach altogether. When we were younger, we didn't have the system of home delivery. As far as tantrums went, you either ate what was there or went to sleep hungry. However, in those days mothers did not have to compete with a hundred different restaurants and fast food centres that have expanded our horizon for food. We used to eat ordinary, staple food happily because every other household made the same things—lentil, rice, vegetables, roti, salad and curd. This was the staple diet and we never cribbed. Like America, now India too is heavily influenced by the fast food industry, changing the way people eat and making us unhealthier by the minute.

But mothers, how do you determine what is right and what is wrong for your child? And how do you cater to the needs of your children, your in-laws and your husband all at once? I bring this recipe book to you to give you just what you need to please not only your picky eater but even your husband and in-laws and, most importantly, YOURSELF. Healthy eating is an important and all too often forgotten aspect of our lives. Why do you think problems like abnormal blood pressure, heart disease and diabetes plague so much of the population these days? I completely understand that in the hustle-bustle of daily life, we tend to forget to take care of our health. I am a working woman myself and I know how hard it is for me to control my diet and make myself go to the gym even though my body is sore. It is difficult without a doubt but, luckily, I know how to cook food that is easy and fast, yet tasty and healthy, so that we don't end up indulging in unhealthy fast food very often.

No matter how many times a child is taught the food pyramid in school, its importance in our life never really sets in. You need to find a way to teach your children first-hand what is healthy and what is not. What better way to do this than by taking them grocery shopping with you? I know it can be a challenging, maybe even unpleasant, experience given how impatient most kids are. However, with the safety and convenience that supermarkets provide these days, it is easier to take your kids along.

These simple yet effective techniques worked wonders with my kids and I hope they do for you too, my troubled readers.

WAYS TO ESTABLISH A HEALTHY FOOD ENVIRONMENT

1. Grocery-shopping with your child

One of the most important things in any relationship is trust. And what better way to instil trust in your kids than by including them in the shopping process? So, as a bonding activity, take them to the supermarket and make them choose what is good and healthy, and cut down on the bottled and canned stuff. It's easier to inculcate good eating habits in them when they develop a sense of healthy and unhealthy food options on their own. If parents who have a busy schedule, cannot do these weekly trips to the supermarket, let the grandparents do this bonding activity with their grandkids. Remember to let your child choose an article from the supermarket—as long as it's something they've never tried before. When they're old enough, give them a little money to buy new food stuff (also a great way of learning quantities and prices).

2. Communication is key

Who was your idol when you were younger? For me, it was always my mom and this is often the case with most kids. From a very young age, children tend to want to be like their parents because they are the primary adult role models. Therefore, even though you might be a busy parent, try to eat at least one meal in a day together as a family. Most importantly, talk about everything but the food during meals since this takes away the kids' attention from the food being eaten. We have a family rule—whenever we go out, or even when we're at the dining table, cell phones need to be deposited at the middle of the table in order to avoid the constant buzz of WhatsApp, Instagram, Snapchat, phone calls and SMSes. This habit of teenagers can be a pain in the derrière; I know how hard it is because my two teens are obsessed with their smartphones. When we are in a restaurant, the person who picks up his/her phone first is the one who pays the bill. Since they don't want to give up their pocket money, meal-time is a happy, no-tech zone.

3. Growing small herbs and plants at home

Growing a few ingredients at home is also a good way for you and your kid to bond. Small herbs like tulsi, basil, cherry tomatoes and lemons are easy to grow in pots and this makes it exciting for the kids because they will be interested in eating the food they grew, plucked and washed themselves. This strategy was helpful not just in my children's case but mine as well. I recall an incident when I was young. We had a *mirchi* (chilli) plant at home and a big mango tree within the building complex. Every time there were nice mirchis in my potted plant and *kacchi kairi* (raw mango) growing on the tree, I would sit with my aunt and learn how to make pickles for the family. I know this generation is not interested in pickles but other home-grown food stuff might catch their fancy.

4. Working in the kitchen with your child

Make meal preparation a time for fun and working together. Let your little one add ingredients to dishes, sprinkle herbs, or stir in the milk. Measuring out a teaspoon of liquid is good balancing practice and adding 4 teaspoons calls on counting skills too. Give your child a board and a plastic grater for some cheese or ask them to chop a courgette with a child-friendly knife available in the market. If you can cope with the initial spillages, letting them get the family drinks will help develop their coordination.

Younger children will love washing up, tearing up salad or getting messy with some floury dough. If the meal is a success, celebrate by inviting one of their friends around and cook it again. Home-made pizzas are great for boosting their vegetable intake and they'll love picking toppings. Fajitas are another alternative.

For instance, my son likes to make eggs in the morning because he enjoys breaking the shells and it's an easy, fun process. So involve your children in cooking small things. Even something as simple as boiling pasta for dinner will go a long way in teaching your children the right and wrong kind of food.

5. Give-and-take relationship

Reward systems can really help in encouraging children to try new food or to do their chores. They can be really effective when it comes to combating picky eating. For younger children, try using a sticker chart: give a sticker for trying something new or for finishing a plate of food. Reward a completed chart with a treat; this should be something small and affordable, not an unhealthy food!

Slightly older children could be given an empty jar to fill with something like dried pasta. Each time they finish their meal or try something new, they get a pasta shape to put in their jar. Once the jar is full, a small present or treat can be given as a reward.

Another way to ensure that your child eats healthy is to bribe them in a way they will never resist. What is the universal love of the world? *Drum roll* Chocolate. So the next time your little ones aren't eating their veggies, just tell them they will get an ice cream or a chocolate later and watch in awe as the greens quickly vanish from their plates. In fact, you can bribe them in other ways too. Having said that, food is one of the few things that children have some control over. So if your child can see that kicking up a fuss about it gets a rise out of you or, even better, a sweet treat, they'll carry on behaving that way. It's very tempting to offer your child food treats just so she 'eats something'. But if you offer fatty, sugary or salty snacks as substitutes, your child might start refusing healthier food. After all, she'll know there are tastier options!

Offering unhealthy treats as bribes can also encourage your child to develop a liking for the treat more than the healthier option.

When my daughter was little, I used to tell her that if she didn't eat her roti and subzi, she would not get the new Barbie doll that she wanted so badly. She would promise to eat everything and stood by her word, on most days anyway.

6. Sitting and eating as a family

It's a good idea to turn off the TV at mealtimes and talk to each other instead. Sometimes toddlers are too distracted to sit at the family table for a meal. If this sounds like your child, you can try having a quiet time before meals so that she calms down before eating. Even the ritual of handwashing can help. Eat as a family. Children learn by example and if they see you enjoying your meal, they are more likely to follow suit. If you can't eat with them, sit with them. If their interest flags, help them by spooning their food. Make mealtimes a happy, social occasion. Try not to worry about knocked-over drinks or food on the floor and give positive feedback on the habits you want continued. Try not to focus on just the negatives.

7. Start in the early years

Imbibing good habits takes time and the sooner the kids learn, the longer they will remember. Avoiding wastage of food is an important lesson they must learn. Therefore emphasize the importance of serving oneself only as much as one can eat. Keeping salads and raitas at the table every day will encourage kids to actually try them. They should also help out in the kitchen—tossing a salad or simply serving the food will encourage them to eat healthier and not waste anything. It's all about the aesthetics, at least according to me, so make your food look appetizing. You can have cutlets with veggies in them but instead of deep-frying them you can pan-fry them and also use olive oil instead of ghee and butter. Avoid monotony and commotion and create a peaceful atmosphere.

Food preferences are developed early in life, so do offer variety. Likes and dislikes begin forming when kids are babies. You may need to serve a new food on several different occasions for a child to accept it. Don't force a child to eat, but offer a few bites. With older kids, ask them to try a bite.

8. Set a good example

Children learn what's healthy and tasty by watching what their parents eat.

So you can set a worthy example by eating the kind of food you would like your child to eat—if you aren't eating any vegetables, your child's not likely to either. Inculcating good eating habits in your child from an early age will make them more likely to continue to follow a healthy régime as they get older.

9. Reduce temptations

Try not to keep junk food around the house. That way, when your child does eventually feel hungry, there will only be healthy snacks available. If you want to keep some snacks, try using a snack jar to limit the intake of these around mealtime.

3

Interest, Taste and Appearance

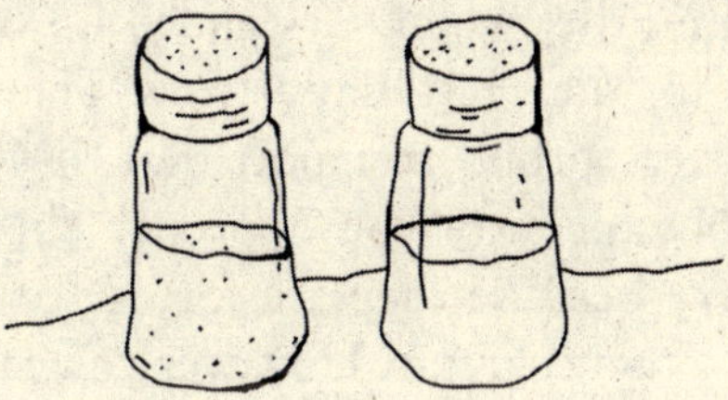

THESE DAYS, NUTRITION is of utmost importance. Since the introduction of fast food chains in India, you have to admit that our eating habits have changed drastically. This is not only because it is cheap and affordable or quick and tasty. According to me, it is also because eating fast food is a huge fad. This is capitalized on by large companies whose practices are primarily profit-driven. What most people don't realize, however, is that fast food is fast for a reason. Have you ever seen a roasted chicken cook in less than an hour? The answer is a resounding 'no'.

The McChicken burger takes less than 2 minutes to make and serve. Have you dug deep and found out why this is so? Cooking is my passion and I can tell you that fast food is not food, it's plastic. I remember when my kids were little, we always ended up ordering from McDonalds for their birthday parties. They used to love it but I am very proud to report that they hate it now. It is all about the way you approach this issue. Most kids are picky because they are forced to eat fruits and vegetables by their parents. However you can ensure that your child eats healthy without the use of force. Making food aesthetically appealing increases the chances of your kid's acceptance of it.

When I faced this problem with my kids, I set about doing some serious thinking. That is when I came up with the idea of replicating fast-food chain fare at home.

Yes, it is absolutely possible to make healthy food at home that is still restaurant-like in taste and appearance. Here, I have constructed recipes that not only provide adequate nutrition but are also quick and easy to learn.

Making food look appealing is just as important for kids as it is for adults. Looking at and thinking about food is the first and, some would argue, the most important stage of digestion.

If the food looks attractive and fun, children are far more likely to want to eat it. Giving individual portions helps make food more appetizing and can also make a meal seem less daunting. Mini versions of classics like shepherd's pie, baked in small dishes such as ramekins, are always popular. This is a great way to cook a large quantity as you can freeze single portions for use at a moment's notice. Children also like to assemble their own food. Lay out a variety of ingredients for your child to put together. This works well with wraps or pizzas. Where a whole fruit may be ignored, threading bite-size pieces on to a skewer or straw will make your children pick them very enthusiastically. Making food preparation interactive in this way enhances the experience.

If your child loves burgers, nuggets and chips, get him to help you make your own junk food. Try making pizzas with tortillas or muffins as the bases, or burgers using good quality, lean, minced meat. Make chicken nuggets by marinating some chicken and coating it in breadcrumbs or crushed cornflakes or Rice Krispies. And how about making ice lollies from fresh fruit and pure fruit juice? There are lots of ways to get your picky eater interested in food. Hopefully, the recipes that follow will help. Remember, you're not alone. Keep trying and good luck!

When she was growing up, my daughter loved cutlets and she would gobble up McDonald's burgers with ease. So I started making vegetable cutlets rather than just the potato ones. The carrots and beans would add extra nutrition. Another option I would offer—a staple in

Sindhi houses—was *saibhaji*, a lentil preparation power-packed with greens and veggies, the leftovers of which would turn into an amazing cutlet. And for the restaurant experience, I would make burgers out of fresh mince and then crumb-fry them to boost the taste factor. If you do this, you will soon find that not only do your kids look forward to mealtimes at home, they also invite their friends over to share this fun experience. For a mother, this is a victory like no other. I realized that home has to resemble a restaurant, menu-wise, so I just made some changes in preparations. For example, instead of serving roti-bhaji, I transformed it into a wrap or a roll which was a great hit with the kids. You can spruce up any roll by adding cheese to it or, if you want, even a nice dip.

For example, a gobi paratha with dahi sounds very boring. Instead, make a *lachha* paratha (multilayered flat bread) with a combination of flour and wheat *atta*. Roll in your gobi aloo bhaji. Make the onion tomato masala like a sauce by blending it. Drizzle some over the roll and serve it with a nice dip. The winning stroke here can be the dip. Make yours with yoghurt, cheese spread, grated cucumber and a bit of seasoning and let them dig into this fun raita. You have won the battle of health and nutrition.

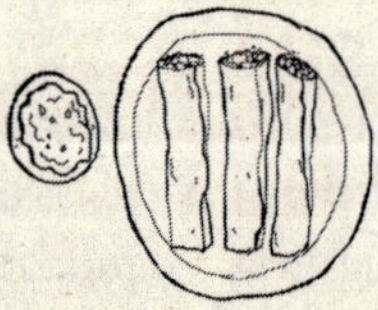

4

Good Food vs Bad Food

I KNOW BALANCING healthy and tasty sounds like a hard goal to achieve but it's actually quite simple. With a few alterations in your regular cooking process, you can achieve great success.

The balancing act starts right from the stage of shopping and it would be great if you could make the supermarket trip a fortnightly outing with your picky eater.

Try barley in winter. This humble grain is amazing when added to soups, or even for a creamy risotto. Your kids are sure to love it because barley has a lovely texture to it.

Pasta is another nice way of introducing freshness into food and is undoubtedly better than the packaged stuff. Involving the kids in the dough- and pasta-making process is a lot of fun and you can do it even when they are as young as seven or eight years old. Making your own jams and chutneys with seasonal fruits like mango and strawberries gives you an amazing spread for breads and toasties for your little ones and packs both taste and health.

FOOD GROUPS AND WHY THEY ARE ESSENTIAL

Have you seen this pyramid before? Do you remember your science class where the food pyramid was taught to you? Now you see it in your child's science textbooks as well. Here, I am going to show you the right way to use this food pyramid. Most people don't know how much or how little to eat of particular food groups which in turn results in wrong and sometimes even dangerous eating

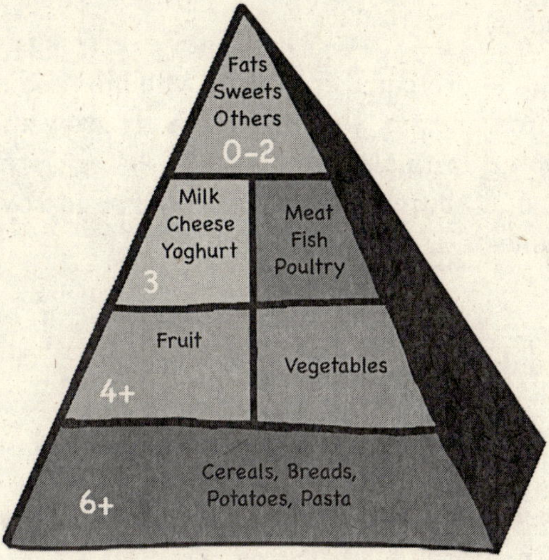

habits. So, just like a tour guide, I am now going to bore you with a lesson on this monument:

The food pyramid

Starchy food

Starchy food contains carbohydrates and B vitamins, with the wholegrain ones being a great source of fibre. Some examples are pasta, potato, rice, oats, bread, cereal, sweet potato, noodles, couscous, green banana, yam, millet, barley and rye.

Consume 3–5 servings of it a day. Portions are to be spread over the day and eaten with each meal (including snacks).

Protein

Food high in protein also contains vitamins and minerals such as iron and zinc that help the body grow and repair itself. Some examples are meat, fish, eggs, vegetable protein, nuts, beans, peas, lentils, corn and soya. Take 2–3 servings a day at least.

Milk and dairy products

Milk and dairy products contain calcium, protein, vitamins including B12, A and D, and can help to keep bones and teeth healthy. Milk, cheese, yoghurt, fromage frais and milkshakes come in this category. Take 3 servings a day.

Fruits and vegetables

Fruits and vegetables provide vitamins, antioxidants and fibre. They can be enjoyed fresh, frozen, tinned, dried or as a juice. Take at most 5 servings a day.

Fats and sugars

Food high in fat and sugar are energy-dense but can be lacking in other nutrients. 'Good' fats or unsaturated fats in appropriate quantities are a great source of fat-soluble vitamins such as vitamins A, D and E. Examples of this category of food include butter, margarine, cooking oils, cream, salad dressings, chocolate, crisps, sugary soft drinks, sweets, jams, cakes, puddings, biscuits and pastries. Avoid indulging in too many or too much in this group, only in moderation as a treat.

THE BATTLE OF THE OMEGAS

Have you heard of omega-3 and omega-6 fatty acids? I am sure you have. Here is a small science lesson anyway. Basically, omega-3 and omega-6 are two types of fatty acids which differ slightly in their chemical structure. These are polyunsaturated fatty acids that our body needs and that can be obtained through our diet. Both work in opposition—omega-3 reduces inflammation, blood clotting and cell proliferation, while omega-6 increases these functions. However, both are required in small amounts for proper functioning of our hormones. According to doctors, the ratio of these two fatty acids should be 1:1. But with the introduction of packaged food, omega-6 has become predominant in our diets. In a survey conducted in America and Europe, the ratio of omega-6 to omega-3 was 10:1 and 12:1 respectively. This is unhealthy and leads to hormonal imbalance in our bodies. Omega-3 is said to have properties that prevent many ailments like heart disease, diabetes and even cancer. This dietary imbalance might explain the rise in the incidence of asthma, coronary heart disease, many forms of cancer, autoimmune disorders and neurodegenerative diseases, all of which are believed to stem from inflammation in the body. The disturbed proportion of omega-3 and omega-6 fatty acids can also lead to obesity, depression, dyslexia, hyperactivity and even a tendency towards violence.

Here is a chart to show you which food contains omega-3 and which omega-6.

Oil	Omega-6 Content	Omega-3 Content
Safflower	75%	0%
Sunflower	65%	0%
Corn	54%	0%
Cottonseed	50%	0%
Sesame	42%	0%
Peanut	32%	0%
Soya bean	51%	7%
Canola	20%	9%
Walnut	52%	10%
Flaxseed	14%	57%
Fish*	0%	100%

SUPERFOODS. WHAT'S THAT?

Let's bring out the wretched science gun again. Superfoods are nutrient-dense whole foods that have high amounts of micronutrients and other unique compounds with incredible healing potential. You may think these are hard to find, but it's quite the contrary. In fact, some of these superfoods can easily be found in the market. For example, did you know spinach was one?

Like a superhero, superfoods can play a major role in rescuing a picky eater. I know families in which one child is extremely choosy about his food while his siblings are serious meat lovers! Some kids also have cibophobia—a scientific term which means fear of food.

It can be a real test to get a picky eater to finish his meal and I sympathize with parents who have to do it every day. This is exactly why superfoods are a blessing—they are a stress-free, low-cost way for your kids to get nutrition despite not being able to eat a large amount.

Although there is no single determining factor to classify something as a superfood, these are typically whole foods which are left in their clean, untreated form. They can be high in either mineral content or vitamins, or in phytochemicals and antioxidants. Superfoods are typically low in saturated and trans fats, are not highly processed and don't contain a lot of food additives.

The definition of a superfood is 'a food considered especially nutritious or otherwise beneficial to health and well being'. With so many unhealthy, processed foods in the market, knowing what superfoods are is an important step in making healthy choices.

Many superfoods are not kid-friendly, so here are some delicious choices that your children will love!

Blueberries

These delicious berries have the highest antioxidant count compared to all other fruit selections. Eating loads of blueberries every day has been shown to lower your chances of type 2 diabetes. Blueberries are also a favourite snack of children because of their amusing shape and great flavour. Serve blueberries on their own when they are in season. Frozen blueberries are a great option for the winter months when it can be difficult to find fresh produce at an affordable price. Freezing doesn't damage the antioxidants so you can feel good serving this fruit.

Oatmeal

Oatmeal is a great breakfast food for children. It's filled with soluble fibre, keeping your kids full for the long hours in school. Oats are also high in protein which makes them a hearty meal on their own. Make this superfood even better by topping a big bowl of oatmeal with fruits, nuts and spices. Leftover oatmeal can be made into oatcakes that your kids will love.

Almonds

These popular nuts are more than just a great snack. Almonds are high in vitamin E and magnesium which can keep your children's cardiovascular system working at peak efficiency. Almonds are also high in healthy fats and antioxidants. The skin of the almond contains over half of the antioxidants, so keep them on and avoid the blanched versions. Serve sliced almonds on top of oatmeal or cereal to get kids to eat this healthy superfood. But be warned. Nuts contain a lot of omega-6 fatty acids and hence going overboard with them is ultimately bad for you. Four almonds are ideal for a child per day.

Eggs

Eggs are a healthy alternative to breakfast cereals. They are fast to cook so they make a great weekday meal. Egg whites are filled with protein and the yolk has healthy fats. Eggs are also high in vitamin B12 and folate. Don't worry about getting high cholesterol from eating egg yolks. Studies have found that people with healthy diets can actually lower their cholesterol by eating eggs. Feed your children scrambled eggs or a healthy omelette to get them to eat this superfood. You could also give them eggs indirectly if they don't like the taste of it. Waffles and pancakes are an easy and sure-shot way to ensure that your kid's diet includes this superfood. Forget kids, who doesn't love pancakes with maple syrup?

Cinnamon

This sweet and savoury spice is a great topping to oatmeal and other confections. Cinnamon is a great hit with kids because of its Christmassy flavour and spicy touch. This superfood has been shown to help stave off colds and flu, and has natural antiviral properties. It's almost calorie-free so it is also a guiltless treat. Your kids will love sliced apples sprinkled with cinnamon for a healthy snack. Because of its sweet taste, you can reduce the amount of sugar you add to oatmeal if you use cinnamon in it.

Grapes

Grapes are a very popular flavouring for children's food products. This is a real fruit that tastes like candy! Filled with antioxidants and polyphenols which give them their rich purple colour, kids love eating grapes right from the stem. The texture is jelly-like, resembling jujubes. Since concord grapes are in season for a very short period of the year, 100 per cent pure grape juice is also a great option.

Strawberries

Strawberries are one of the top antioxidant-containing fruits available in the market. These delicious berries are loved by children because of their mild sweet flavour. They are also high in iron, making them a great snack. Strawberry season can be short but you can generally find them round the year. Dried strawberries make for a delicious treat as their texture becomes similar to chewy candy. They are also sold frozen across stores.

Yogurt and milk

Greek yogurt is a top superfood because of all the protein and calcium you get in each serving. This thick, creamy treat comes in different flavours and fat content. Most varieties are 2 per cent fat, but you can also find completely fat-free versions. Flavour it yourself with honey and fruit, or buy pre-flavoured ones. Your kids will love having this as a snack or even for dessert and you will love knowing they're getting tons of calcium and protein with every bite.

Delicious and healthy, milk is another great way for kids to get calcium. Skimmed milk is low in calories but high in protein and delivers a ton of calcium. However latest studies have found that children should drink whole milk instead of the skimmed version. The extra healthy fats are better for them in the long run and in case they are allergic or intolerant to milk, there are amazing nut milks and soy milk products available in most grocery stores.

Fitness trainer Yasmin Karachiwala's favourite recipe for fussy eaters:

Vegan Chocolate Mousse

- Take one ripe avocado and puree it until it's smooth.
- Now, take ¼ cup of cocoa powder and coconut/almond milk each and mix the two together. Then add them to the avocado.
- Now take 2 teaspoons of a natural sweetener/stevia and 1 teaspoon of natural vanilla extract and add both to the above mixture.
- You can also add nuts or berries if you want to give your dessert that extra crunch or flavour.

Transfer the mixture into individual bowls and refrigerate them until cold.

Combining superfoods in kid's meals with foods they already know and love is one of the simplest ways to give them super nutrition. Take my blueberry banana spinach smoothie for example. It's sweet and delicious and a cheat's way to introduce superfoods in their daily diet since they will not be able to taste the spinach and be none the wiser!

Blueberry Banana Spinach Smoothie

Spinach might sound strange in this recipe but you won't even notice it since the blueberries mask the taste. Spinach fulfils 40 per cent of your daily need for vitamin A and 25 per cent for vitamin C, among many other nutrients.

Serves: 1

Ingredients

Frozen blueberries – 1 cup
Banana – ½
Skimmed milk – ½ cup
Baby spinach – ½ cup
Honey or agave – 1 tbsp
Vanilla extract – ½ tsp
Ice cubes – 4

Method

Place all the ingredients in a blender and chop until smooth. Serve immediately.

TIPS FROM THE TOP

That last item on the list might have conjured up some ghosts for some of you. I am assuming that most parents face an issue when it comes to making your child drink milk or trying to make them eat yogurt. Many children simply do not like milk, no matter how many ads promise everlasting bone strength and no matter how many other children eagerly gulp down a glassful. Children and even adults who don't like milk often complain that it smells horrible, tastes appalling and it makes them sick knowing where it comes from. Some kids detest milk so much that simply being close to it is sufficient to induce nausea.

Well, the fact of the matter is that milk is essential for your child, whether he/she likes it or not. So here are a few tips from me on how to make your child drink milk.

- ***Chill it*** Cold milk tends to go down way easier than hot milk. Some say it reduces the smell and is, therefore, more bearable.
- ***What type of milk is it?*** Full fat milk can sometimes be undesirable, so try giving skimmed or semi-skimmed milk to your child. Some kids when given almond or soy milk prefer it to regular milk. So there are alternatives, don't worry!
- ***Flavour it*** If you can, then why not? Blend some milk with bananas to make a smoothie

or add milkshake powders or syrups to it. If you are a health-conscious mummy, then replace the sugar in the smoothie with dates or even honey. Use cocoa powder instead of artificial milkshake powders and use more fruits. Healthy can be tasty!

- ***Drink it right out of the carton*** Some kids enjoy the thrill of drinking flavoured milk from the tetrapack. So try it out.
- ***Ignore it*** The other sure-shot way is to ignore that you're having milk. Make your child drink it like medicine by pinching their noses. This might help lessen the impact of its taste since the senses are connected. Also tell them to try and gulp it down real fast and not to let it linger in the mouth since it tastes worse that way. Another option is to simply provide milk masked in a cake or cookies.
- ***Soak it up with another food*** You all have seen the Oreo ad. Give your child some cookies and let them dunk away. This way, they will consume at least some of it!
- ***Minimize it*** Pour very little milk in some cereal and use a really small glass to drink from. Just take small sips at a time. That way the taste won't be too prominent.
- ***Chase it down with something yummy*** If you tell your child to drink the milk fast and then eat a chocolate or a cookie afterwards, it will help wash down the taste of the milk.

- ***Substitute it*** If you, as a parent, absolutely need your child to obtain the calcium and other nutrients present in milk, then you should go to a general physician or nutritionist and get a calcium tablet or find other ways to substitute this drink. Many other foods, like capsicum, are also high in calcium; however, chewable gummy bears and orange-flavoured tablets are a better option considering capsicum is probably an even bigger no-no for your kid.

5

Common Food Aversions

MANY TIMES, WE as parents face picky behaviour only for some parts of the day or, in fact, a couple of food items.

How many of you have children who absolutely hate milk? Or green leafy vegetables? Or, in some cases, even eggs and meat?

There is a way to deal with each and every one of these aversions. The reason for dealing with them is that your children need these nutrients, whether they like the taste or not.

Children are expected to complain about certain food items and say things like, 'I don't eat eggs, ever,' or, 'Sprouts! Eww, gross!' However, if this problem persists and actually makes it to adulthood, it needs a very valid health-related, political or environmental argument to support this aversion—a severe allergy is even better. If you don't like a particular food, you may seem like a picky child to your friends and this isn't something you want to deal with on business dinners. Do you want your children to grow up and become an adult with a job and a spouse but still fuss about food like a ten-year-old? You wouldn't want them to go on a date and seem unadventurous and unhealthy because they only order junk food even at the age of twenty-four, would you?

I am guessing you will say no. Most adults develop these food aversions during childhood which eventually turn into phobias. In fact, foods many people hated when they were growing up not only provide essential nutrients for adult bodies but also house a potpourri of savours, tangs and zests.

We all know children are often reluctant to eat their veggies, so the trick is to find ways to 'sneak' them into their food. Here are the most common 'ick' foods that are actually incredibly good for you—and tasty as well—and tricks to include them in your child's meal.

1. CAPSICUM

Capsicum comes from the Americas and is a genus of the flowering plants in the nightshade family. Now it is cultivated everywhere in the world. These colourful fruits (yes, I said fruits) are beautiful and sweet and have different names everywhere (like bell peppers, chillies and so on). The green and purple varieties are slightly bitter. However, the red, yellow and orange varieties have a sweet and refreshing taste.

Health benefits

These fruits are rich in vitamin C, even more so than any citrus foods. They also have antioxidants and phytonutrients in abundance. Capsicum has most of the vitamins of the B complex range, even an abundance of vitamins A and E. It has anti-ageing, cancer-preventing and even anti-bacterial properties. It also aids in keeping cholesterol in check and enhances the body's metabolism.

Learn to like it

'How do I include capsicum in my child's diet?' you must be wondering. It's not that hard, actually! One way to include capsicum in your food is through rice. Chop up a few into tiny cubes, toss them with some herbs and olive oil and sauté them. Add the rice and toss again.

Accompanied with a yummy sauce, your children won't even realize that they are eating capsicum! Speaking of sauces, just puree a capsicum of any colour with some water and stir it into your white sauce to make it healthy. This makes it colourful and elevates the taste. Stuffing the capsicum with potatoes, rice, kidney beans, salsa, cottage cheese, chicken or any other filling you like, and then baking it in the oven is another brilliant way to mask its taste and still provide the required nutrition.

2. BROCCOLI

It is a staple of popular culture that kids loathe broccoli and kick up a mighty fuss when forced to eat it. The vitamin K in these shrub-like plants is what you would like your children to obtain. Children hate these flower-shaped greens (and others in its family of cabbage) probably because they are not as yummy as chicken nuggets or a bar of Snickers. However, broccoli can be made into a treat too. It is easy to prepare and can be made into a delicious side dish or even tossed in a summery salad.

Health benefits

This flower-like vegetable has superlative amounts of vitamin C and dietary fibre. It also has moderate amounts of vitamin K and A. Besides that, broccoli is known to contain many nutrients which possess potent anti-cancer properties, like diindolylmethane, and traces of selenium. Just one serving gives you more than 30 mg of vitamin C. Diindolylmethane also fights other viruses and bacteria.

Learn to like it

Why do you want to avoid the good stuff? You can always skewer these babies with some other veggies and marinate them in spices for flavour. They even go well with dips like hummus or with some ranch dressing. Make a tasty potato and broccoli soup and add some yummy croutons so your kids will love it; grate some parmesan on top to make it even yummier. You can crumble the florets to put in a salad of your choice or even in mince pies and *tikki*s. You could always keep it simple and just steam or bake them with olive oil for a quick side dish. If you want to get exciting, cover a casserole dish with broccoli. Then pour 3 tablespoons of butter over it and season with pepper and salt. Sprinkle some cheddar cheese on top and then bake for 10–15 minutes.

3. FISH

Most children fuss about this particular food group the most. They find everything wrong with seafood—fishy taste and smell, slimy texture, the constant paranoia that you might swallow a bone and so on. However, it is a real shame to not enjoy the sea's bounty because it prevents you from eating some yummy dishes from multiple ethnic cuisines. Not only that, it is the perfect protein source to help you lose weight and cut down on meat with saturated fat.

Health benefits

Fish is a lean protein and contains many other vitamins and minerals. The main minerals include selenium, zinc and iodine. Selenium is an antioxidant and has anti-cancer properties. Iodine is great for a healthy metabolism, while zinc helps to boost the body's immune system. However, the most important element present in oily fish is omega-3 fatty acids. Like I mentioned before, our body requires these healthy fats for early development of the brain and nerves. The term 'brain food' is used to describe exactly this kind of food group. Fish also contains many vitamins like A, E and even D, which one usually gets from the sun.

Learn to like it

Most kids think that all fish have the same taste—extremely fishy. If you as parents aren't going to expose them to different kinds of fish, how will they ever know otherwise? You can do this with baby steps and give them something they are guaranteed to love, like fish fingers or fish and chips. These dishes are a food favourite and will be a hit with your kids as well. However, if you aren't too keen on these fried options, try to begin with these and then move on to fish in Chinese sauces or curries. Remember that perseverance is the key. Salmon is the best option for this recipe as it's the healthiest, but you can also use rawas or tilapia. You can always test whether your child likes shellfish such as prawns and crab. That's also a start!

4. BEAN SPROUTS

Sprouts are the soft, edible shoots of certain plants. Though *moong* bean is the most commonly used bean sprout, there are many other seeds that can be sprouted.

For example, lentils, alfalfa seeds, kidney beans, sunflower seeds, peas, white beans and even adzuki beans. For centuries, bean sprouts have been eaten for their amazing health benefits. These can be eaten raw in a salad or cooked. Sometimes people even put them in juices. The taste differs from sweet to bitter depending on the type of seed.

Health benefits

Bean sprouts are highly nutritious and tend to retain their beneficial properties until consumed, unlike other vegetables which start losing their nutrition the moment you pluck them. These shoots contain all the vitamins—A, B, C, D, E and K. They are a rich protein source (excellent especially for vegetarians) and also contain a lot of fibre which aids digestion and is good for people suffering from constipation. Apart from this, sprouts contain minerals like folate, potassium, iron, phosphorous, magnesium and zinc. They can be good for kids with anaemia or a low haemoglobin count because of their high content of iron. It also keeps cholesterol in check, has anti-ageing properties, reduces stress and even strengthens hair and nails. Their importance for your kids cannot be stressed enough.

Learn to like it

Bean sprouts can be added to tikkis and also to salads and raitas. With enough perseverance, your kids will learn to like them.

5. BEET

No matter how vibrant the colour of this vegetable, beet still remains unappetizing to many adults and children alike. I understand that it can be hard to know what to do with them. When cut, beets look like slices of bloody meat. However, their sweet taste and bright, blood-red colour can dress up a salad.

Health benefits

These red babies are actually high in carbohydrates. They are a quick energy source without the weight you gain from processed carbohydrates. Beets are also a wholesome source of magnesium, niacin, iron and calcium, along with vitamins like A and C. Many studies have shown that they reduce the risk of colon cancer.

Learn to like it

Like I said earlier, beets go well in a salad. However, if you aren't too keen on salads, you can always put it in a soup to get a vibrant red colour. You can also blend it with hummus to make a funky snack.

6. SPINACH

Beets and spinach come from the same family which almost guarantees that your child will dislike it. No matter how much Popeye loved this vegetable and how much your kid likes Popeye, getting him to emulate his favourite cartoon character's spinach-eating habit is impossible. The leaves are long and broad with a smooth texture and a bitter taste.

There are many types of spinach and they grow slightly differently everywhere, but they taste almost the same.

Health benefits

Just like the other vegetables outlined previously, spinach also has vitamins A and C, lots of fibre, magnesium, folic acid and many other nutrients which helps prevent cancer, particularly of the colon, lung and breast. It also reduces the risk of heart disease. So this veggie is something that your child needs for great blood building, stronger gums, clear and good eyesight and a healthy bone structure.

Learn to like it

Most kids crib about the bitter taste of spinach but this can be masked quite easily. The one good thing about this vegetable is that it can be cooked in many ways. Why don't you try adding a blanched spinach layer to your lasagna? Your child will love this dish because it's super cheesy and yummy and it will still have the nutritious value we want to give to them. You can try putting it in a fruit smoothie, like I told you in Chapter 4. Like capsicum, it can also be pureed and put into white sauce. You can always put spinach as a topping in a pizza, inside a quiche, or even add it to a yogurt and cheese dip.

7. EGGPLANT

Eggplant or aubergine or brinjal belong to the same family as capsicum—the nightshade family. The most common type of eggplant is glossy, smooth-skinned and teardrop-shaped and has a dark purplish, satin-like peel. Inside, its spongy flesh is white or creamy-white and has many small, edible seeds. This dark fruit comes in other shapes like long or thin and its colour can vary too. They can be white, white with red stripes and even green, like the Asian Pea eggplant that is used in Thai curry.

Health benefits

It has all the nutrients, vitamins and minerals that the previously listed vegetables contain. It has abundant vitamin B6; only 75 grams of eggplant provides for the daily requirement of vitamin B6. This helps the blood, brain and other body functions.

Learn to like it

Eggplant has established itself in many cuisines worldwide, even though it originated in China. Many cuisines have signature dishes in which the eggplant is the star. Many Indian dishes have eggplant, like *baingan ka bharta*. However, for someone who has a picky eater at home, a good way to incorporate eggplant in food is to either fry it or put it in sandwiches, or make a yummy dip after roasting the eggplant.

6

'I'm Not a Kid, Mummy!'

MANY YOUNGSTERS ARE picky diners. But picky eating isn't always about food—it's often about children wanting to be self-determining. Here are some ideas to help with your child's picky eating habits.

Try making sure that your child gets all meals and snacks at a regular time each day. If they are not hungry in between meals, you can even try to get rid of snacking.

If your child is really hungry when meals are placed on the table, you can cheer them on and help them satisfy their appetite by offering more food. On the other hand, if they are not very interested, it is completely all right if they eat less—they might be hungry again at the next meal, or at snack time.

Setting a time limit for mealtimes will encourage your kid to eat faster because when kids eat leisurely, they tend to play around and waste more food. When the time is up, take the plate away. Your child will actually ask for it back. This is a good way of making sure that they finish quickly the next time.

The less you discuss your child's eating habits, the better it is. Such discussions could lead to an argument at the dining table. Your child's food acceptance partly depends on the ambience created. When eating in a stressful environment, kids tend to take it out on their food.

It's also advisable not to have unrealistic expectations. For instance, you can always ask your child to try all the food on his plate or at least a couple of spoonfuls of each item.

If you have a toddler, try encouraging them to sit at the table, even if it's on a high chair and for a short while. You can always increase this time period as they get older and become more patient.

Provide your child with choices within the range of healthy foods you offer but try to keep the options limited to two or three things only. Otherwise they become too confused or dazed to eat. For example, instead of asking them to pick what they want from the fridge, ask, 'Would you like grapes or cucumber?'

It can be a good notion to support your child's need for individuality when it comes to what they want to eat. It won't hurt anyone to take the crusts off their bread if that's what the child wants. If you give in to a few demands or preferences, you'll help them feel more in control. Remember this, though—you are the one who decides what your child eats but they can decide how much.

If you put a small amount of each food item on the plate, it will ensure that they don't feel overwhelmed.

While doing all this, keep in mind that perseverance is the key. You should never give up. If you offer the same food item multiple times, your child is more likely to try it and eventually like it. In fact, they might have to see a certain type of food on the plate 10–15 times before accepting it. It doesn't even matter if your child doesn't take the first step in accepting new food items. Continue to offer it at other times of the day and other days of the week as well.

Whenever possible, try and make your child share snacks and even meals with their friends. They might be more willing to try a new food if other children are also enjoying it.

And as much as possible, try not to serve different food to your kids and the rest of the family. If your child doesn't want to eat it, say something reassuring like, 'It's so tasty, I love it.' If they still don't want it, say calmly, 'Okay, you can try it another time when you're hungry.'

It's a good idea to try and serve your child something new at every meal along with something they like to eat. This way, the effect of yummy and healthy is balanced and your child is more likely to eat both if given in small and equal amounts. For example, a piece of boiled broccoli alongside some potato wedges is sure to be a hit.

Inculcating a sense of intrigue in his food can encourage your child to try it. Therefore encourage him to touch, smell or take a lick of the new food item, then applaud them for giving it a try. The next step is to urge them to take a bite. Keep the applause going . . . children want to please their parents and this little effort will motivate them to go on.

Children also like to emulate their parents. So along with them, you must also eat a variety of nutritious foods at each meal. And go for variety yourself—show your child that you're willing to try something new and enjoy eating it.

Getting used to mealtimes, new foods, strange textures and flavours can be upsetting for a child. Similarly, spending a lot of time cooking food that is almost always left untouched, desperately cajoling your child into sitting at the dining table, or forcing them to try at least a single bite, can also be frustrating for a mom or dad.

Feeding off your responsiveness, a child's unease can manifest itself as obstinacy or even belligerence, setting the stage for a mealtime spectacle.

Just take a deep breath and relax. If you are getting worked up about your child's dietary intake, stop. Recent American research suggests that even the pickiest of young eaters are likely to meet or exceed their recommended energy and dietary intake at their age. So try focusing on giving your child a healthful, nourishing upbringing instead.

The same research goes on to say that chances of a toddler accepting a new food item only increase after we've offered it to them more than eight times. If the answer is still 'no', try to mask your frustration. Tell them that it's really sad that they are not eating it because their grandmother—*dadi* or *nani*—loves it, and you think that they're really missing out on the yummy stuff. Make 'taking a bite of everything on my plate' or 'sitting at the table until I'm finished' categories in your child's reward scheme. Remember that positive attention and praise are the best rewards.

Whenever you're cooking for a picky eater, try not to spend too much of your time and energy in making food which they probably won't eat. I want you to promise me that you will not spend more than 10 minutes preparing food for the little brats! Trust me, the less effort you put into making it, the less hurt you'll feel when it goes into the garbage bin.

It is a truth universally acknowledged that food will be a stress-inducing problem for parents at least once in their child's life, even if it's for a short while. However, getting angry and expressing it as a means of disciplining your child is the wrong way to go about it. I am not asking you not to get angry; I'm not a counsellor. All I am saying is to mask it. I know that being harsh and firm can get your child to eat their meal, probably even finish it. However, you need to know that now your child dreads mealtimes more than ever. This is because fear has been added to disgust. Anger is a very natural reaction but it's important to deal with it. Remember that your children also learn from you. If you keep yourself calm, they will follow suit and learn to control their anger.

Having said that, if you feel your child is not receiving the required intake of vitamins and minerals, then go to a doctor and get some prescriptions for nutritional supplements. You don't need to be too concerned; your child's body will get the nutrition it requires one way or another. There is no need to panic if the only form of protein your child had was a glass of milk or chicken sausages.

7

Importance of a Family Routine

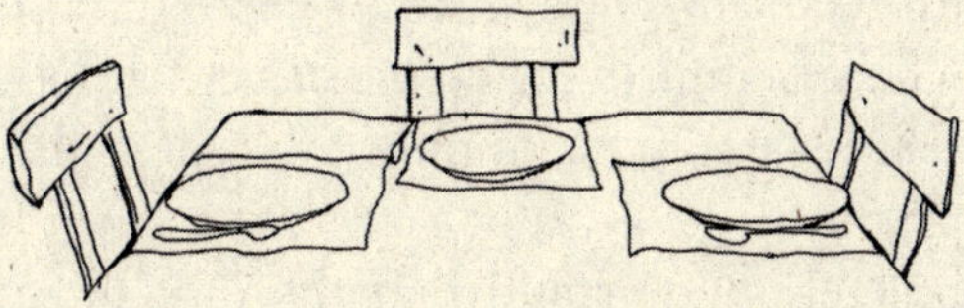

ALL THE ADVICE in this book is derived from my personal experience. A fixed family routine for mealtimes has brought my family closer and I am so sure it will do the same for everyone. It made my family accustomed to seeing each other at mealtimes and the cribbing about hunger reduced since everyone knew when they were going to get food.

Benefits of a routine

It is said that families that follow a daily routine tend to have healthier kids. My children started to behave better once I enforced this routine and sleeping and eating on time even helped improve their grades in school. Also, the little time we spent at the dinner table brought us much closer.

I completely understand that the thought of making a routine which includes all the activities of the day like meals, study time, TV time, chores and so on can be really terrifying and time-consuming. However, once you make the effort and the kids settle down in the schedule, you don't have to worry about picky eating. You and your kid will fight less at mealtimes. Isn't that motivation enough? With a set routine, everyone knows what needs to be done when. This prevents unnecessary conflict between parents and children.

For the first two weeks at least, write the routine on paper and stick it up on the fridge. This way, everyone who walks up there sees the schedule and follows it. You can take it down once the family has grown accustomed to it and committed it to memory.

How to set up a routine

Worrying as it may seem, setting up a routine is really quite simple. Just begin by observing your family members' sleeping patterns and then centre the meal plan around that.

Be realistic, however, and allow enough time for your children to bathe and get dressed, especially if this is new for them.

Also, you must allot time for extra things to be done in the routine. This includes the basic needs of a family like chores, study time, TV time, and so on. If you have more than one child, try to spend quality time with them individually during the day. Some kids have after-school activities like swimming or karate and some have tuitions and such, so don't forget to mention it in the schedule so you know who to pack a snack for and who is going to be home at what time.

Very importantly, focus on the night-time activities and make sure that all the chores of the day are done. For example, the homework should be completed in a timely manner during the day, schoolbags for the following day should be packed in advance and uniforms should be laid out the night before. You need to make sure that your children do all of this in order to not mess up the routine by sleeping late or going to school late.

Whenever you can, try to include your partner in doing the chores and spending time with the kids as well. It is understood that this can be hard for a working mother or father but concerted attempts to participate jointly in family activities help the child trust both of you instead of leaning on just one parent.

Get as many inputs as you can from your family and talk it through with other parents. A meal plan and a routine that everyone likes will cause less conflict and ensure that it is followed.

If there's a single activity, like brushing of teeth, which is a nightly sticking point, set up a Reward Chart to deal with it, or add this chore to your child's existing chart.

When you first introduce the routine, rest assured you will hear some cribbing from your kids. Make sure that your partner and you are on the same page and talk them through everything in a firm manner while still being open to their opinions and the changes they would like to make. I can assure you that soon your kids will be the ones reminding you to stick to the schedule. And trust me, that is a great feeling.

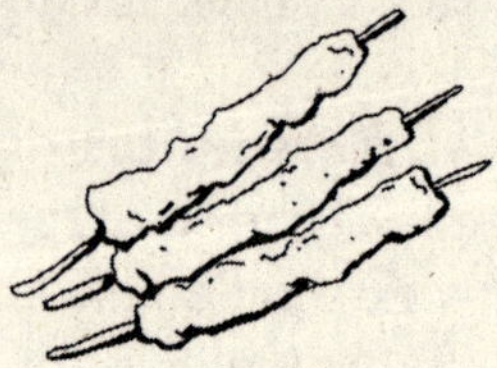

8

How to Stay Calm with Your Picky Eater

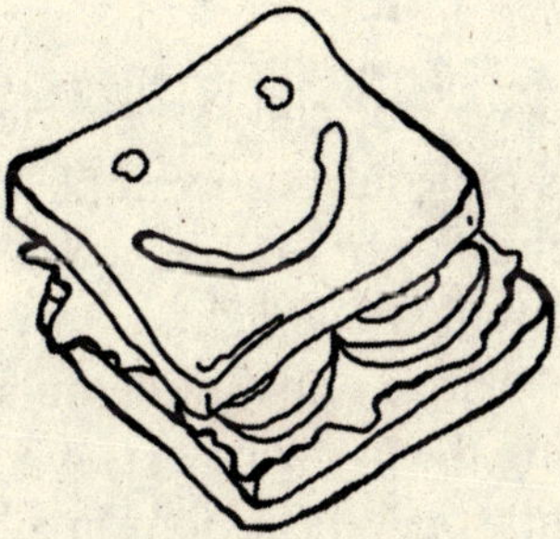

BEING A PARENT is a worthwhile and pleasurable experience. However, it can also be demanding and infuriating. It's just as hard as any other job, probably even more so. To add to that, if our child is always fussy about food, we tend to lose our composure and flip out despite wanting to resolve it calmly.

What can we do to prevent this? How do we keep our cool when all we want to do is scream at them when they say 'Just chill'? My son and daughter would say this to me all the time! The key is not to get angry.

Here are three sure-shot ways in which you can change your entire life (exaggerating a tad, but if you are a parent, this is a substantial chunk of your life!).

1. CHANGE THE WAY YOU VIEW YOUR CHILD'S BEHAVIOUR

The way you view your child's behaviour will influence the effect it has on you. For example, if you think that wasting a few bites is not that big a deal, you will be able to avoid a potentially huge fight.

How do we change our views, you ask?

Understanding the development of a child can aid you in seeing your little one's behaviour in a less negative light. This technically means that you must not think of your child's behaviour as a personal bad habit, but as the way all kids behave. This way, you won't be overly harsh on them.

Parents frequently complain, 'She's riling me up' or 'She knows how to push my buttons.' If you truly think that your child is purposely trying to upset you, then you are wrong.

Try letting go of the idea that your infant or toddler is conspiring on how to drive you crazy. I was talking to a friend of mine who is a counsellor and she told me of a concept in developmental psychology called 'theory of mind'. She explained that this kind of manipulation is developmentally impossible as it requires a child to be able to understand that other people have beliefs and intentions different from their own.

This comparatively advanced type of thought progression does not develop in children until around the age of three or four.

So why don't you just try to view your toddler for what he or she is? A little human being looking at the world with a brand new ability to move around and a simple desire to explore everything around them. Remember that the little human being causing such mayhem can't understand that his or her actions affect other people. They have not yet developed self-discipline and so will act on a whim. Being unaware of the concept of time, your toddler will be impatient as well.

As for an older child who you feel is intentionally winding you up, try to see why they are acting that way. Perhaps they have learnt that driving you to the brink of your patience is the only way to get what they want? Make sure that your child receives your attention for all the positive behaviour you want to see more of.

2. TRY TO REDUCE STRESSFUL MOMENTS

Reducing the number of stressful altercations you have with your children over food will lead to a happier atmosphere at home. Children tend to readily absorb the emotional climate they are in—if you're stressed out and sour-faced, they will be too.

I completely understand that it can be hard to keep your tone polite, calm but firm. Using clear, brief, simple commands will help you. Children can, and surely will, pick up on any hints of stress, wavering or anger in your voice and this might make them more agitated or even more persistent.

Although it is tempting and sometimes inevitable, avoid being sarcastic ('Wow, I love this! It's so much fun cleaning up your mess!'), threatening ('Trust me, I will leave if you don't hurry up'), judgemental ('You only think of yourself') or overly critical ('Why do you always have to be so lazy?'). Remember that in the short term, such comments will trouble and irritate your child but in the long term they may cause a corrosion of their self-confidence.

Most parents are aware of the need to praise a child's good behaviour. However, frequent frustrating encounters with their children can make them reluctant to praise the latter on the rare occasions when it is deserved. I strongly advise you not to fall into this trap. Positive reinforcement for good behaviour is essential to a child's development. To make it easier, you could try setting small, easily achievable goals. For example, praising your kids even if they finish only half of their food will encourage them to try more next time.

Also, consider agreeing to a fixed number of house rules and penalties. You could have a coin jar so every time your kid does something that wasn't meant to be done, he puts a coin in it. So that it seems fair, involve yourself in this activity as well . . . it will also give them a chance to enjoy catching you in the wrong! You could write these rules down and stick them up on the fridge.

Most importantly, set aside some weekly relaxation time for yourself. This is not just a treat but also a requirement. It may be a massage, a nice walk, listening to music or just a long bath. Arrange for a babysitter (preferably a grandmother) and just enjoy whatever little freedom you can get.

3. HOW TO COPE WHEN CLOSE TO SNAPPING

Why?

When you react in anger, it leads to rash and irrational decisions. Sometimes you can also become aggressive with your child and respond by shouting, hitting, or even punishing them in the heat of the moment. But how do you feel about it in the end? Remorseful and disturbed, isn't it? Your child also gets affected and feels frightened. Harping on the point yet again, it's natural to get angry but you can't let anger control you.

How?

You can pick up on the clues that your body gives you when you're getting angry. For example, a racing heart, shaking limbs, sweating and so on.

The moment you notice your body's signals, stop wherever you are and pause what you are doing. Then try to look at the issue in a rational manner without letting the anger surface. This will always help check your anger.

Don't ever forget to express your feelings to your child. If spoken to nicely, they will definitely understand.

Try to avoid getting into an argument as much as you can. Show that you want to resolve the issue but, at the moment, you need to be alone in order to cool off.

If you can leave your kid under someone else's care to get some space, do so. Remove yourself from the situation and go away for a bit.

I know this might sound like yoga but deep breathing can really help calm a person down. Take deep, long breaths through your mouth and exhale through your nose. Also, while breathing in, try to clench your fists tightly. Unclench as you exhale slowly. This will calm you down further and reduce your chances of responding with anger.

If getting away from a volatile environment is not possible, use a different method to distract yourself. I usually count backwards from ten to one in my head. People who love music can try singing their favourite song, or if you are one of those who find solace in writing, then write away. You could also channel your anger in a task that requires aggression, like cleaning the house, or going to the gym.

Basically, do whatever it takes to stop yourself from reacting rashly. You must be positive and say to yourself, 'I'm really calm' and that 'This too shall pass.'

Remember, pent-up anger can result in an unexpected outburst later, so express it in a different way.

If these methods don't help, there is no shame in seeking professional advice. Stress and anger can have an adverse effect on one's health and, therefore, should be dealt with seriously.

Don't forget that as the parent, you hold the reins. What you buy and what you cook is not always going to be what your child wants to eat. Stay strong through all the pestering and cribbing. Getting used to the 'I hate this' and 'I hate that' is a smart move, and the sooner you realize this, the better. Try to give the kids what they want at least once a week so that they start to tolerate the nutritious food you serve most of the time. Keep healthy snacks in the fridge and kitchen cupboards so that they have no choice in the matter. If you want, you can keep a few of their favourites stocked, just so they don't feel depressed.

Be careful when offering your children food if you don't want them to rebel against you. They should also have a say in the matter. Whatever you offer them, let them have the freedom to decide how much of it they want to eat. Like I said earlier, having a meal plan or schedule will ensure that your child is hungry at appropriate hours. Include them in the schedule-making process so they feel like they have a say in the house. I know that sometimes you just feel like giving in but don't go soft by letting them take advantage of the freedom that you give them. If you follow my advice, your kids will slowly get accustomed to their schedule and their complaints will also reduce. Every kid has a different appetite so try to make sure that they serve themselves as much as they would like to eat without wasting. That way, they will also not end up overeating.

It's advisable to inculcate good habits at a young age. Start replacing junk food with tasty yet healthy food right from the beginning. For example, give your kids an egg salad sandwich instead of a hot dog or burger, or, some pesto pasta instead of macaroni and cheese. When going out for dinner, make them try new and different types of dishes instead of what they are used to. This way, they feel more adventurous and will not restrict themselves to the same kind of unhealthy foods.

Calories in drinks count. Soda and other sweetened drinks add extra calories and get in the way of good nutrition. The best and least harmful drinks for our kids are water and milk. I have already told you in Chapter 4 how to deal with a milk aversion. Juice is fine when it's been freshly squeezed but kids don't need much of it—4 to 6 ounces a day is enough for preschoolers.

Food is not love and should not be communicated as such to a child. Find better ways to say 'I love you.' I suggest you rethink the strategy of rewarding your kids with their favourite food because it forms subtle emotional associations for them. These, in turn, give rise to child obesity. Instead of showing love through treats like chocolates and ice cream, or gifts and toys, give them a warm hug or a kiss.

PART TWO

Recipes

1

Breakfast

BREAKFAST IS THE most important meal of the day and I am only here to guide and provide all you concerned parents with easy recipes that not only your picky eaters but also the rest of the family will love.

What does breakfast consist of? What should it consist of? How do you provide your child with a healthy breakfast? I am sure these questions run through your mind every day before waking up your little ones. Well, most of the cereal available these days is so full of sugar and preservatives that it is only tasty but has no nutritional value. There goes one of the most popular breakfast items! So what can you do?

No worries. I have a lot of power-packed recipes that are just perfect for your little one to kick-start his or her day with. The main reason we eat breakfast is not only because we are breaking a fast but also because there is science behind it. It is said that having a hearty breakfast aids in a faster metabolic rate and also helps you avoid excessive snacking during the day.

I think breakfast should have a little bit of everything—some protein, some carbohydrates and of course, some fibre. So essentially, a glass of milk or a fruit shake is a great accompaniment to breakfast and is easy to make as well. Along with a milkshake you must also give a protein like egg which is the perfect way to start the day and can be served in many ways. Muesli or oats can also be a great source of fibre.

Apart from the usual ones, I have constructed some unique breakfast dishes that will make your picky eater eagerly await this mealtime every morning. Let's hope you enjoy cooking these dishes for your little ones as much as I loved putting them together.

Dahlia Upma

Serves: 4

Ingredients

- Dahlia/broken wheat – 1 cup
- Onion – 1 small, minced
- Tomato – 1, chopped
- Carrot – 1, grated
- French beans – 2–3, finely minced
- Curry leaves – 8–10
- Mustard seeds – ½ tsp
- Asafoetida – ¼ tsp
- Jeera – 1 tsp
- Green chilli – 1, slit
- Salt – to taste
- Haldi – a pinch
- Coriander leaves – 2 tbsp, chopped
- Ghee/butter – 1 tbsp

Method

1. Boil the dahlia in 1 cup water and salt for 5–10 minutes or till the water has dried up and the dahlia is cooked.
2. Heat ghee in a kadai and add mustard seeds, let it splutter and add the jeera, curry leaves, asafoetida and stir for a few seconds.
3. Next add the onion and fry till slightly pink; add the beans and grated carrot and stir for a minute.
4. Add salt, a pinch of haldi, green chilli, chopped tomato and finally the dahlia and stir well.
5. Cover and cook on a slow fire for 5–7 minutes or till done. Garnish with coriander leaves and serve.

Eggs Benedict with Hollandaise Sauce

Serves: 6

Ingredients

- Buns – 3
- Bacon strips – 2–3
- White vinegar – 2 tsp
- Eggs – 6
- Clarified butter – 5½ tbsp
- Egg yolks – 2
- Salt – ½ tsp
- Lime juice – few drops
- Pepper powder – ¼ tsp
- Butter – to spread
- Fresh parsley – chopped, for garnish

Method

1. Take 80 gms of butter and heat in a deep pan. This helps the solids separate. Remove the scum from the top. Switch off the gas and let it settle down. What you are left with is clarified butter on top.
2. Beat the egg yolks on a double boiler and add the clarified butter little by little, stirring constantly with a wire whisk or wooden spoon. Gradually add the lime juice. Keep stirring until it thickens. Your hollandaise sauce is ready. Add salt and pepper before serving.
3. Brown the bacon in a medium pan. Toast the buns and butter them.

4. Take a 10-inch non-stick pan and fill with water till it is half full. Add white vinegar. This will make the egg white cook faster so it does not spread. Bring to a slow boil. Gently break one of the eggs into the water (using a ring mould) taking care not to break it. Repeat with remaining eggs. Reduce the heat to a gentle simmer. Cook for 3½ minutes until the egg white is set and yolk remains soft. Remove with a slotted spoon, allowing the egg to drain.
5. Lay a slice of bacon on top of each buttered bun, followed by a poached egg. Season with salt and pepper. Spoon hollandaise sauce over the eggs. Garnish with chopped parsley.

Chef's Tip

Using a ring mould helps the eggs poach better in a circle and not spread all over.

Calorie Control

Worry not mommies, you can use Nutralite instead of regular butter and add a touch of creamy spinach to enhance the nutritional value.

Alternatively, I sometimes prefer to serve some smoked salmon with this and my kids simply love it. So you could give it a try as well.

Banana Pancakes

Serves: 2

Ingredients

- Flour – 200 gms
- Baking powder – 1 tbsp
- Baking soda – ½ tsp
- Salt – ½ tsp
- Sugar – 30 gms
- Egg – 1
- Milk – 1 cup (200 ml) skimmed milk /buttermilk
- Butter – 1 tbsp, melted
- Bananas – 2, mashed
- Maple syrup – as required
- Whipped cream – as required

Method

1. Mix the flour, sugar, baking powder, baking soda salt in a bowl and keep aside.
2. In another bowl mix the milk, butter, egg and mashed bananas.
3. Add the flour mixture, taking care not to over mix it.
4. Heat a flat griddle or pan over medium-high heat.
5. Spoon drops of 1½–2 tbsp of the batter on the hot griddle and when bubbles appear on the surface of the little pancakes, flip them over to make them golden brown on both sides. A minute or so on each side should do it.
6. Serve hot with maple syrup and some whipped cream.

Chef's Tip

Add milk according to the size of the bananas. The batter should have a thick consistency like dosa batter. Alternatively, you can use a handful of blueberries instead of bananas.

Calorie Control

I prefer to use egg white instead of the whole egg. Also you can opt for skimmed milk or buttermilk, or even almond milk—the latest healthier option rich in protein and less on calories. Try this switch and trust me, they won't even know the difference. In fact they may like it better.

Spanish Omelette Frittata

Serves: 4

Ingredients

- Olive (not virgin) oil – 3 tbsp
- Onions – 1 medium sized, sliced
- Eggs – 4
- Potato – 1, sliced
- Garlic – 1 tsp
- Fresh parsley – 2 tsp
- Fresh thyme – 1 tsp
- Bell peppers (red, yellow, green) – ¼ each, sliced
- Salt and pepper – to taste
- Cheese – ½ cup, grated

Method

1. Slice onions and bell peppers into thin strips. Set aside.
2. Grate the cheese and set aside.
3. Peel the potato and cut it in half lengthwise, then slice into thin half-moons.
4. Heat an oven-proof non-stick pan of 4–5-inch diameter over medium heat and add 1 tbsp oil.
5. Sauté the garlic and onions for a few minutes till they are soft and golden.
6. Season with the herbs and add salt and pepper to taste.
7. Stir together, cook for a few more seconds, then transfer to a bowl. Add the remaining oil and heat the pan until very hot.

8. Add the potato slices in batches and cook on both sides until cooked through.
9. Drain on paper towels. Remove excess oil from the pan.
10. Arrange the potato slices in a fan pattern so they completely cover the bottom of the pan.
11. Carefully arrange the vegetables over the potatoes. Place the pan on the gas over low heat.
12. Beat the eggs in a bowl, season with salt and pepper and mix well. Carefully pour the eggs over the potatoes. Cook for 30 seconds or so, then sprinkle the cheese on top and transfer the pan to the oven.
13. Cook for about 20 minutes until the eggs are set. To serve, loosen the edges of the frittata with a spatula, then place a plate over the pan and carefully invert so the potatoes face up. Slice into wedges and serve.

Parmesan Herb Mini Muffins

Serves: 6

Ingredients

- Flour – 125 gms
- Baking soda – ½ tsp
- Baking powder – ⅛ tsp
- Melted butter – 42.5 gms
- Egg – 1
- Buttermilk – 142 ml
- Parmesan cheese – 50 gms
- Mixed herbs – 1 tsp
- Dry basil – ½ tsp

Method

1. Preheat the oven at 180 degrees.
2. In a bowl, mix flour, baking soda, baking powder, parmesan cheese, mixed herbs and basil.
3. In another bowl mix melted butter, buttermilk and egg.
4. Now mix together the dry and wet ingredients and make a thick batter. Do not overbeat.
5. Pour this mixture in mini muffin trays. Bake for 15–20 minutes.

Chef's Tip

These can be cut through and used as mini muffin sandwiches which would be perfect for a party.

Parmesan Herb
Mini Muffins (p. 80)

Banana Pancakes (p. 76)

Spanish Omelette Frittata (p. 78)

Elvis Banana and Peanut Butter Sandwich (p. 83)

Healthy Muesli (p. 84)

Eggs Benedict with Hollandaise Sauce (p. 74)

Dahlia Upma (p. 73)

Sua Idli (p. 81)

Sua Idli

Serves: 4

Ingredients

- Urad dal (split black lentils) – 1 cup
- Ukda chawal (parboiled rice) – 3 cups
- Methi (fenugreek) seeds – ½ tsp
- Salt – to taste
- Sua (dill leaves) – a handful
- Garlic –2–3 cloves, minced
- Green chillies – 2, minced
- Oil – for greasing the moulds
- Coconut chutney – to serve with
- Sambhar – to serve with

Method

1. Soak the urad dal and fenugreek seeds together in ample water for 3 hours and drain.
2. Soak the rice in enough water for 3 hours and drain.
3. Blend the urad dal and fenugreek seeds together in a mixer till smooth and frothy (add water little by little as required). Remove and keep aside.
4. Blend the rice in a mixer till smooth. Remove and keep aside.
5. Combine the urad dal paste and rice paste together in a bowl, cover and keep aside to ferment overnight.
6. Once the batter is fermented, add salt, chopped sua, green chillies and minced garlic to the batter.
7. Put spoonfuls of the batter into greased idli moulds and steam for 10–12 minutes.

8. Repeat with the remaining batter to make more idlis. Serve hot with fried coconut chutney and sambhar.

Chef's Tip

You can use store-bought batter and just add the garlic, chilli and sua to it. I love sua pankis. A spinach puree instead of the sua can be a healthier option.

Elvis Banana and Peanut Butter Sandwich

Serves: 1

Ingredients

- Multigrain bread slices – 2
- Butter – to spread
- Peanut butter – to spread
- Banana – 1, chopped
- Maple syrup – to drizzle
- Cinnamon powder – ½ tsp

Method

1. Butter the slices well and spread peanut butter generously.
2. Add the chopped banana and drizzle some maple syrup. Add a dash of cinnamon powder.
3. Grill in a sandwich griller till crispy and brown. Slice and serve these heavenly toasties or sandwiches to all your picky eaters.

Healthy Muesli

Serves: 10–15

Ingredients

- Oats – 250 gms
- Cranberries – 100 gms
- Almond flakes – 100 gms
- Sunflower seeds – 25 gms
- Pumpkin seeds – 25 gms
- Raisins – 50 gms
- Walnuts –25 gms
- Black currants – 25 gms
- Brown sugar – 100 gms
- Honey – 8 tbsp
- Butter – 50 gms, melted

Method

1. In a bowl, mix the oats, almonds flakes, raisins, black currants, pumpkin seeds, sunflower seeds, cranberries and walnuts.
2. Add the brown sugar and honey.
3. Mix well. Add the melted butter.
4. Put it in a greased tin/silicon mould.
5. Bake it at 140–160 degrees for 35 minutes or till the muesli is nice and golden.

Calorie Control

Using brown sugar is healthier than white sugar as brown is raw and unrefined. Honey can also be substituted with melted jaggery (the quantity would be 2 tbsp less).

Crumpets

Serves: 4

Ingredients

- Warm milk – 175 ml
- Flour – 225 gms
- Yeast – 2.5 gms
- Sugar – 5 gms
- Warm water – 175 ml
- Salt – 2.5 gms
- Baking powder – 2.5 gms
- Oil/butter for greasing

Method

1. Whisk together the milk, flour, yeast and sugar. Add the warm water slowly to this until the batter is thick and smooth. Stop adding water once it reaches a thick creamy texture. Cover with cling film and leave in a warm place to foam.
2. Once the batter has foamed, whisk in the salt and baking powder. Allow to stand for 10 minutes.
3. Dampen kitchen paper with a little oil and grease the base of the pan.
4. Place ring moulds in the heated pan, add enough batter to fill just below the top of each ring. Cook for 5 minutes on one side, then flip it and cook on the other side.

Chef's Tip

I learnt to make crumpets in my bakery training class. Britain's favourite breakfast option, they are a must-try and can be served with jam. They will be a little sweet but won't do any harm.

Creamy Scrambled Eggs

Serves: 2

Ingredients

- Eggs – 6
- Milk/cream – 4–5 tbsp
- Salt – to taste
- Pepper – to taste
- Butter – 1 tbsp
- Oil – 1 tsp

Method

1. Mix the eggs and milk or cream in a dish and keep aside.
2. Heat oil and add butter, then pour in the egg mixture. Season with salt and pepper.
3. Keep stirring and gently lifting the eggs from the bottom of the pan and cook until still creamy and soft. Take it off the heat and serve on toasted bread with a side of hash brown.

Chef's Tip

I prefer milk to cream for a lighter effect.

2

Lunch

DON'T YOU JUST hate it when the lunch box you packed at 7 a.m. comes back untouched? Well, I think it's high time now this trend changed.

Let's face it. Very few parents have the time and energy to pack a new and exciting lunch for their kids every single day. We know the struggle involved in putting together breakfast and dinner and, on top of that, if you're stuck with a picky eater who needs a surprise in the lunch box every day, how can we cope?

Don't worry. I have a set of perfect, quick and easy recipes here to make your lunch box chore much easier.

So what can you pack for your child that you are sure will be eaten? Nowadays due to the compartmentalization of lunch boxes, you can put in dry and wet food separately. But you can't really pack your child dal, chawal and subzi. It's just really messy and doesn't remain hot until lunch hour.

So I suggest you put in a mix of things in the lunch box. Put one dry sandwich or wrap which serves as the main. Then in one compartment you could put a few slices of cucumber and carrot which serve as a salad. In another smaller compartment, put a yummy dip (for example hummus, yogurt dip, barbeque sauce). A juice carton is a great way to wash it all down. For dessert you can always give a fruit or some chocolate. Now that wasn't so hard, was it?

Lebanese Wrap with Hummus and Chips

Serves: 4

For the falafel

Ingredients

- Dahlia – 100 gms
- Breadcrumbs – ½ cup
- Chickpeas – 200 gms (soaked overnight and pressure cooked. It should be of a mashable consistency.)
- Lime juice – 1tbsp
- Garlic – 2 tsp, minced
- Coriander leaves – 2 tbsp, minced
- Parsley – 2 tbsp, minced
- Paprika – 2 tsp
- Cumin powder – 1 tsp
- Salt and pepper powder – to taste
- Baharat – 2 tsp (Baharat is a Lebanese spice mix easily available in stores)
- Mini pita pockets – 8–10

Method

1. Soak the dahlia in warm water for 15 minutes and drain. Keep aside.
2. Add the chickpeas, dahlia, lime juice, breadcrumbs, garlic, coriander leaves, parsley, paprika, baharat, cumin powder, salt and pepper powder. Check for seasoning.
3. Wet your hand and shape into small, flat cutlets.
4. Fry in oil till golden brown.

For the hummus

Ingredients

- Chickpeas (canned) – 1
- Tahina paste – 4 tsp
- Garlic – 4 cloves
- Olive oil – 4 tbsp
- Paprika – 1 tsp
- Lime juice – 2 tbsp
- Cumin powder (optional) – 1 tsp

Method

1. Combine the tahina, chickpeas, garlic and lime juice, and make a smooth paste.
2. Drizzle olive oil on top.
3. Sprinkle paprika powder.

To assemble

Heat the pita bread on a tawa and place the falafel and hummus with some cucumber, lettuce and tomato on a plate. Serve with chips.

Chef's Tip

I prefer to use dahlia which is more accessible than burghul in India. Alternatively you can substitute with quinoa and, instead of deep-frying, you can bake these in an oven. Bake at 170 degrees for approximately 20 minutes or till crispy.

Calorie Control

I came across the air fryer quite accidentally and found it to be a great boon in our kitchen where there is always something to fry. But the trick is that it can dehydrate the food, hence it takes lesser time. So go ahead and try these in an air fryer. You can even try them in the oven; only, it will take longer.

Teriyaki Chicken and Veggie Noodles

Serves: 2

Ingredients

- Boneless chicken (leg portion) – 100 gms, shredded
- Noodles – 1 packet, boiled
- Peppers (red, yellow, green) – ¼ of each, sliced
- Broccoli – 3–4 florets, blanched
- Spring onion (white and green) – 1, sliced
- Zucchini – 3–4 slices
- Bean sprouts – a handful
- Garlic – 2 tsp, minced
- Teriyaki sauce – 2 tbsp
- Oyster sauce – 2 tbsp
- Soya sauce – 2 tbsp
- White pepper powder – ½ tsp
- Salt – to taste
- Oil – 2 tbsp
- Eggs – 2, scrambled

Method

1. Heat 1 tsp oil in a wok and add chicken; season with salt and white pepper powder and keep aside.
2. Heat 1 tsp oil again and season the scrambled eggs with salt and pepper and keep aside.
3. Heat remaining oil and fry the garlic and all the veggies except the bean sprouts. Stir for a few seconds.

4. Next, add the chicken, eggs, noodles, teriyaki sauce and oyster sauce and season well. Stir on a high flame for a minute.
5. Switch off the gas and add the sprouts. Toss well and pack the noodles with a small container of soya sauce for extra punch.

Chicken or Veg Fricassee with Butter Parsley Rice

Serves: 1

Ingredients

- 1 chicken breast
- Onion – medium size, ¼
- Mushrooms – 3–4
- Butter – 1 tbsp
- Flour – 1 tsp
- Dry white wine (optional) – 15 ml
- Chicken stock – ½ cup
- Amul cream – 30 ml
- Thyme – a sprig
- Nutmeg – a pinch
- Salt and pepper – to taste
- 1 cup cooked rice (a day old and kept in the fridge)
- Parsley – 1 tsp, minced
- Mixed herbs – a pinch

Method

For the chicken fricassee:

1. Cut the chicken breast into long strips about 1 cm wide. Then toss them in flour until fully covered.
2. Dice the onion and mushrooms.
3. Heat the butter in a frying pan and cook the onions until soft.
4. Add the mushrooms to the onions and cook for 3–4 minutes.
5. Add the chicken, cook until brown all over.

Chicken or Veg Fricassee with Butter Parsley Rice (p. 96)

Lebanese Wrap with Hummus and Chips (p. 91)

Palak Paneer Paratha (p. 105)

Oatmeal and Raisin Cookies (p. 111)

Vegetable Sandwich (p. 108)

Spaghetti Alio Olio (p. 107)

Teriyaki Chicken and Veggie Noodles (p. 94)

Oats and Moong Dal Tikki Frankie (p. 101)

6. Pour in the white wine and boil to burn off the alcohol. Add the sprig of thyme, and salt and pepper to taste.
7. Add the chicken stock, bring to a boil and simmer for 20 minutes.
8. Remove from the heat and add the cream. Then put it back over the flame and warm it, taking care not to let it boil.
9. Serve on a bed of butter parsley rice.

For the butter parsley rice:

1. Heat butter in a pan and quickly toss in the rice with parsley and herbs and season well to serve as an accompaniment with the chicken fricassee.

Chef's Tip

You can substitute chicken with mixed vegetables and continue with the same recipe. I prefer to use olive oil for the rice but you could switch to rice bran oil as a healthier option. I have tried it and it works just fine.

If some mothers are apprehensive about using wine, they can completely omit it. Wine essentially lends acidity to the dish and evaporates once cooked.

Calorie Control

You can use a jowar atta instead of flour and get the same result while coating the chicken.

Paneer Makhanwala Wrap

Serves: 4

For the makhanwala

Ingredients

- Paneer – 100 gms (cut diagonally)
- Flour – 2 tsp
- Cornflour – 3 tsp
- Salt – to taste
- Garlic paste – ½ tsp
- Red chilli paste – 1 tsp
- Baking powder – a pinch
- Sugar – a pinch
- Oil –1 tsp, for frying

Method

1. Marinate the paneer pieces in a mixture of all the ingredients for 15 minutes and fry them.

For the wrap

Ingredients

- Multigrain atta – ½ cup
- Wheat flour – ½ cup
- Flax seed powder – 1 tsp
- Salt – to taste
- Milk – 3 tbsp
- Water – as required
- Oil – for brushing
- Lettuce

Method

1. Knead the ingredients (except oil and lettuce) into a soft dough, brush oil and keep aside to rest. Milk makes the dough soft.
2. Make roti wraps out of this dough. For a healthier version, cook on a tawa and keep aside.
3. Place paneer and some lettuce on the wraps and roll them. Serve the makhanwala sauce on the side since pouring it on the wrap will make it soggy and your picky eater will send the lunch box back, untouched.

For the makhanwala sauce

Ingredients

- Onion – 2, sliced and browned (check tip for browning below)
- Almonds with skin – a couple of handfuls
- Red chilli paste – 2 tbsp (check recipe in basics)
- Ginger–garlic paste – 1 tbsp
- Tomato ketchup – 2 tbsp
- Tomato puree – 2 tomatoes
- Kasuri methi – 1 tsp (dry roast on tawa)
- Coriander powder – 2 tsp
- Turmeric – a pinch
- Garam masala – 1 tsp
- Salt – to taste
- Water – as required for the sauce
- Oil – 2 tbsp
- Cream – 2 tbsp

Method

1. Grind the onion, almonds, red chilli paste and ginger–garlic paste to a smooth paste, adding water if required.
2. Heat oil and fry the paste. Add the tomato puree and ketchup and cook on a simmer.
3. Next add coriander powder, turmeric and salt with kasuri methi and add water if required to adjust the consistency. Finally finish off with garam masala. If you don't have a problem with cream, then add some after you switch off the gas.

Chef's Tip

You can also use a mix of wheat flour and bran flour for your roti wraps. Bran gives more fibre. Feel free to add cheese, it's just irresistible!

Calorie Control

I prefer to use regular oil instead of butter in this recipe especially because we make it once a week.

My next cheat is to use almonds with the skin since it's a dry fruit that we all need on a daily basis. It also lends to the creaminess of the sauce.

You can brown the onion in an oven or the air fryer with just a dash of oil. Voila! You have saved on the extra consumption.

Lastly, you can use Greek yoghurt as it's easily available in stores, or cheat with milk instead of cream.

Oats and Moong Dal Tikki Frankie

Serves: 6

Ingredients

- Yellow moong dal (split yellow gram) – ½ cup
- Quick cooking rolled oats – ½ cup
- Fresh curd – 2 tbsp
- Roasted besan – 1 tbsp
- Green chillies – ½ tsp, finely chopped
- Chaat masala – 2 tsp
- Chilli powder – 2 tsp
- Garam masala – ¼ tsp
- Turmeric powder – ¼ tsp
- Ginger–garlic paste – 1 tsp
- Coriander (dhania) – 1 tbsp, finely chopped
- Onion – 1 tbsp, minced
- Chilli garlic sauce – 1 tbsp
- Salt – to taste
- Oil – 2 tsp, for greasing and cooking
- Roti wraps or tortilla wraps for frankie

For the frankie masala

- Amchur powder – 1 tsp
- Chilli powder – ½ tsp
- White pepper powder – 1 tsp
- Salt – 1 tsp

Method

1. Clean, wash and boil the moong dal in 1 cup of water till it is soft and cooked and all the water has evaporated.
2. Drain and blend the dal in a mixer to a coarse paste.
3. Transfer the paste to a bowl, add all the remaining ingredients (except chilli garlic sauce) and mix well; reserve some oats for coating.
4. Divide the mixture into 12 equal portions. Shape each into a long sausage roll and coat with oats.
5. Lightly grease a non-stick pan with ½ tsp of oil.
6. Cook each roll in the pan with minimum oil.
7. For the frankie masala, mix the ingredients in a bowl and sprinkle on the rolls.

To assemble

Roll the roti or wrap over each cutlet after adding some minced onion and coriander. Serve with chilli garlic sauce.

Rajma and Cheese Paratha

Makes: 4

For the dough

Ingredients

- Wholewheat flour – 1 cup
- Oil – 1 tbsp
- Salt – to taste

Method

1. Combine all the ingredients and knead into a soft dough using enough water.
2. Divide the dough into 4 equal portions.
3. Roll out each portion into a big roti (8-inch diameter, like a pizza).
4. Cook each chapatti lightly on both sides on a hot tawa and keep aside.

For the rajma filling

Ingredients

- Red rajma (kidney beans) – ¼ cup, soaked
- Onions – ½ cup, chopped
- Garlic paste – 2 tsp
- Tomatoes – 1 cup, chopped
- Turmeric powder – ½ tsp

- Chilli powder – 1 tsp
- Coriander powder – 2 tsp
- Coriander (chopped) – 1 tbsp
- Vegetable stock – 2–3 tbsp
- Salt – to taste
- Spring onions – 2–3, finely chopped
- Grated processed cheese – 4 tbsp
- Oil for cooking

Method

1. Drain the kidney beans; add 2 cups of water and pressure cook for 4–5 whistles till the rajma is overcooked.
2. Drain any excess liquid and keep aside.
3. Heat the oil in a pan; add the onions and garlic paste and sauté till the onions are light brown in colour.
4. Add the tomatoes, turmeric powder, chilli powder, coriander powder and salt and cook till the oil separates.
5. Add the cooked beans and mix well. Add 2–3 tbsp stock and continue cooking till the mixture is dry.
6. Add the coriander and mix well. Keep aside to cool. Divide into 4 equal portions.
7. Place one chapatti on a dry surface and spread one portion of the rajma filling in its centre.
8. Sprinkle some spring onions and 1 tbsp of cheese.
9. Place the other roti on top and lightly press together. If the sides are open, then lightly seal them with egg or cornflour mixture (2 tsp cornflour with 1 tsp of water). Repeat to make 3 more parathas.
10. Heat the parathas on a tawa. Once cooked on both sides, apply oil to make it crispy and golden. Serve hot.

Palak Paneer Paratha

Makes: 4

For the palak gravy

Ingredients

- Palak – 1 cup
- Ginger, garlic, green chilli paste – 1 tbsp
- Cashew – 4–5

Method

1. Wash and blanch the palak in boiling water with salt for 2–3 minutes. Strain and refresh in cold water and let it cool.
2. Blend the palak with cashew and ginger, garlic and green chilli paste into a smooth puree (avoid adding water).

For the parathas

Ingredients

- Multigrain atta (store bought) – 1 cup
- Wheat atta – 1 cup
- Salt – to taste
- Haldi – a pinch
- Red chilli powder – ¼ tsp
- Ajwain – ¼ tsp
- Jeera – ¼ tsp
- Water – for kneading
- Ghee – 2 tsp (and some more for the paratha)

Method

Mix all the ingredients and knead into a dough with the required amount of water. Set aside.

To assemble

Ingredients

- Paneer – 150 gms, crumbled
- Onion – 2 tsp, minced
- Salt – to taste
- Amchur – a pinch
- Coriander leaves –2 tsp, chopped

Method

1. Mix onion, salt, amchur, coriander leaves and the palak puree into the crumbled paneer.
2. Make small roundels of the dough.
3. Take a roundel and put some dry atta on both sides, roll into a round disc to the size of a roti. Add 2–3 tsp of the filling and cover from all sides resembling a *potli*.
4. Rub dry atta on both sides and roll it into a stuffed paratha.
5. Heat a hot tawa and cook each paratha on both sides till done, then add ghee and cook for a few seconds more on each side till golden in colour. Serve hot.

Chef's Tip

Sauté all the ingredients along with the palak puree to cut down the taste of iron.

Spaghetti Alio Olio

Serves: 2

Ingredients

- Spaghetti – 100 gms (boiled al dente)
- Olive oil – 2 tbsp
- Garlic – 2–3 cloves, sliced
- Cherry tomatoes – 2–3
- Red chilli – 1, sliced
- Mixed herbs – a pinch
- Parsley – a few sprigs, chopped
- Pasta liquid – 1 tbsp (from the boiling)
- Parmesan cheese – 50 gms (Grana Padano)

Method

1. Gently heat olive oil in a pan, add garlic and switch off the gas. Let the garlic infuse the oil for a minute.
2. Put the heat back on and add chilli, spaghetti, mixed herbs, cherry tomatoes, salt and pepper and toss well.
3. Add the grated Parmesan cheese, some pasta liquid and toss well with fresh parsley. Serve.

Vegetable Sandwich

Makes: 4

Ingredients

- Wholewheat bread slices – 12
- Butter – 3 tsp for brushing
- Cabbage – 1½ cups, shredded
- Carrot – 1 cup, grated
- Paneer – ½ cup, grated
- Processed cheese – ¼ cup, grated
- Coriander – ¼ cup, finely chopped
- Green chillies – 1 tsp, finely chopped
- Mayonnaise – 3–4 tbsp
- Salt – to taste

Method

1. Make a stuffing using the cabbage, carrot, paneer, cheese, coriander, green chillies, mayonnaise and salt.
2. Divide the stuffing into 8 equal portions and keep aside.
3. Apply a little butter on both sides of each bread slice and toast them lightly on a tawa till both sides are golden brown in colour.
4. Place one toasted bread slice on a clean, dry surface and spread a portion of the prepared stuffing evenly over it and sandwich it with another toasted bread slice.
5. Then spread the second portion of the prepared stuffing evenly over it and again sandwich it using one more toasted bread slice.
6. Repeat steps 3, 4 and 5 to make three more sandwiches.
7. Cut each sandwich diagonally and serve immediately.

Tomato and Red Pepper Sauce

Ingredients

- Tomatoes (red and ripe) – 4, skinned
- Red pepper – 1
- Carrot – 1
- Brown sugar – 4–5 tsp
- Chilli powder – 1 tsp
- Onion – 1 small, minced
- Olive oil – 1 tbsp
- Salt – to taste
- Mixed herbs – a pinch
- Veg seasoning – a pinch

Method

1. Heat oil in a pan and fry the onion till light pink. Next add the carrot, red pepper and tomatoes, all finely chopped.
2. Season with salt, brown sugar, veg seasoning, a dash of chilli powder and some mixed herbs.
3. Add water if required and cover and cook till completely softened.
4. Let it cool down, blend and strain. Check the seasoning and serve your own homemade tomato sauce.

Calorie Control

In this recipe we have added all the nutrients—from carrots to red pepper—in addition to the tomato sauce which will give it more colour. The texture of the vegetables is hidden from our picky eater. Plus the brown sugar gives it a natural element and adds to the colour, making it look closer to a store-bought sauce.

Oatmeal and Raisin Cookies

Makes 25–30 cookies of 30 grams each

Ingredients

- Butter – 225 gms, softened
- Flour – 150 gms
- Sugar – 225 gms
- Raisins – 150 gms
- Milkmaid – 400 ml
- Oats – 200 gms
- Cinnamon powder – 1tsp

Method

1. Cream the butter and sugar until light and fluffy.
2. Add Milkmaid, oats and cinnamon powder.
3. Add flour and raisins. Make a soft dough.
4. Roll the dough into even-sized pieces (about the size of a golf ball). Place them spaced out on a greased baking sheet and flatten them with your fingers.
5. Make sure to preheat the oven at 160 degrees. Bake for 15 minutes or till pale brown.
6. Cool on a wire rack.

Chef's Tip

I use a convection oven because it bakes evenly.

3

Dinner

DINNER IS THE last and somehow the most anticipated meal of the day. Everyone in my family waits for dinner excitedly! 'I need some healthy yet delicious ideas for dinner' is the thought that runs through the mind of every mother.

But how do you meet everyone's expectations after a tiring day that was full of chores and slaving over breakfast and lunch? Relax. I've got just what you need. Easy and non-time-consuming recipes for a perfect, restaurant-quality dinner.

Manchow Soup

Serves: 4

Ingredients

- Chicken/ vegetable stock – 300 ml
- Cabbage – 50 gms
- Carrot – 1 small, minced
- Mushrooms – 2–3, minced
- Capsicum – 1 tbsp, deseeded and finely minced
- Tomato – 1 small, minced and without the pulp
- Ginger – ½ tsp, finely minced
- Garlic – ½ tsp, finely minced
- Green chillies – to taste, finely minced
- Oyster sauce – 1 tbsp
- Soya sauce (dark) – 2 tsp
- Salt and pepper – to taste
- Chilli oil – 2–3 tbsp
- Cornflour paste – 3–4 tbsp
- Boiled, shredded chicken (optional) – 60 gms

Method

1. Heat oil in a wok and sauté the ginger and garlic. Next add the stock.
2. Bring the stock to a boil and add all the vegetables, seasonings and sauces.
3. Add the cornflour paste and thicken the soup.
4. Serve the soup in a bowl and garnish with chilli oil.
5. Alternatively, garnish with shredded chicken and spring onion leaves and serve.

Chef's Tip

Everyone loves crispy fried noodles. For this, you can use boiled noodles, drain it on a kitchen paper and then deep fry it. It can be served with the soup. Seasonings and sauces in Asian food means salt, pepper, oyster and soya sauce, in that order.

Calorie Control

You can crisp up the noodles in the oven, brushed with oil, or in the fryer.

Chicken in Oyster Sauce

Serves: 4

Ingredients

- Chicken (boneless) – 250 gms
- Egg – ½
- Cornflour – 2 tsp
- Peppers (red, yellow, green) – ¼ of each, shredded
- Green chillies – 5–7, sliced
- Spring onion – 2–3, sliced
- Ginger – 2 tbsp
- Garlic – 2 tbsp
- Salt and white pepper powder – to taste
- Soya sauce – ½ tbsp.
- Chicken seasoning – 1 tsp
- Cornflour paste – 1 tbsp
- Oil (to fry) – 2 tsp
- Oyster sauce – 2 tbsp
- Chicken stock – ¼ cup

Method

1. Marinate the chicken with ½ egg, 2 tsp cornflour, salt and white pepper powder for 15 minutes. Deep-fry and keep aside.
2. In a wok heat the oil and add ginger, garlic, green chillies and sauté for 1 minute.
3. Add the spring onion, peppers, chicken seasoning, salt and pepper and stir-fry for 1 minute.
4. Add a little stock and sauces, then add the fried chicken.

5. Add the cornflour paste and stir-fry for 1 min.
6. Sprinkle some spring onion greens and serve.

Chef's Tip

All Asian sauces and seasoning contain excess salt, so taste before adding salt.

Vegetable Fried Rice

Serves: 4

Ingredients

- Long grained rice – 250 gms
- Carrots – ¼ cup, finely chopped
- Beans – ¼ cup, finely chopped
- Capsicum – 3/4 cup, finely minced
- Spring onion – 2–3, shredded
- Salt and white pepper – to taste
- Soya sauce – 2 tbsp
- Oil – 4 tbsp

Method

1. Pick, wash and drain the rice. Boil the rice in plenty of salted water till three-fourths cooked.
2. Drain the rice through a strainer and cool under running water. Refrigerate the rice for 1 hour.
3. Heat some oil in a wok and add the vegetables. Stir-fry on high flame. Add the seasoning and soya sauce.
4. Add the rice and fry well. Garnish with spring onion greens and serve hot.

Egg fried rice

Put oil in the wok and add the eggs with salt and scramble. Add the spring onions and stir-fry. Add the rice, soya sauce, salt and white pepper powder. Garnish with spring onion greens. Serve hot.

Non-veg fried rice

Same technique, just add boiled, shredded chicken and/or fried prawns to the rice.

Pan-Fried Noodles

Serve: 4

Ingredients

- Noodles (boiled) – ½ packet
- Carrot – 1, cut diagonally and blanched
- Bean sprouts – ½ packet
- Spring onion – 3, cut diagonally
- Bamboo shoots – 1 tbsp, cut diagonally
- Chicken seasoning –1 tsp
- Chicken stock – 1 cup
- Mushrooms – 2–3, sliced
- Broccoli – 3–4 small, cut into florets and blanched
- Zucchini – few pieces, cut diagonally
- Baby corn – 3, cut diagonally and blanched
- Peppers (red, yellow, green) – ½ cup constituting all three
- Garlic – 5–6 cloves, crushed
- Garlic – 2 tsp, minced
- Oyster sauce – 1 tsp
- Shaoxing wine – 2 tbsp
- Rice vinegar – 1 tsp
- Salt and white pepper – to taste
- Cornflour – 2 tbsp mixed with a little water
- Oil – 4–5 tbsp
- Butter –1–2 tbsp
- Spring onion greens – to garnish, cut diagonally
- Chicken (shredded) – 200 gms

Method

1. Marinate the chicken with 2 tsp cornflour and season with salt and white pepper powder.
2. Boil the noodles in lots of water and salt. Strain and refresh in cold water, put oil and keep aside.
3. Put oil in a wok and stir fry the shredded chicken and keep aside.
4. In the wok put oil, add the garlic and stir-fry. Add all the vegetables.
5. Add all the sauces and seasonings, stir well and add the stock.
6. Let it come to a boil. Add the chicken and thicken it with cornflour.
7. Put a little oil in the wok and stir-fry the noodles with the minced garlic and some spring onion greens.

To assemble

Heat a sizzler plate, add some butter and put a layer of noodles. Let it heat up till golden brown and crispy at the bottom.

Pour the chicken and vegetable sauce preparation on top and serve.

Chicken Satay

Serves: 4

Ingredients

- Chicken – 400 gms
- Coriander seeds –1½ tsp, roasted
- Garlic paste – 3 tbsp
- Lemongrass – cut 2-inch long
- Fresh turmeric –1½ tsp
- Sugar – 6 tsp
- Salt – to taste
- Soya sauce – 6 tbsp
- Lime juice – 6 tbsp
- Oil – ½ tsp

Method

1. Cut the chicken into long strips and keep aside.
2. Grind the coriander seeds, garlic paste, lemongrass, fresh turmeric, sugar, salt, soya sauce, lime juice and oil to make a paste.
3. Marinate the chicken strips with the ground paste. Put them on skewers in a zigzag fashion and refrigerate for 2 hours.
4. Heat a grill, brush the chicken with little oil and grill for 6–8 minutes.
5. Serve with peanut sauce.

Peanut Sauce

Serves: 4

Ingredients

- Peanuts –100 gms, roasted
- Tamarind pulp – 1 tbsp
- Brown sugar –1 tbsp
- Onion – 1 small
- Garlic – 2 cloves
- Red chillies – 6–8, soaked
- Coconut milk – 1 tsp
- Oil – 1 tbsp

Method

1. Heat the oil in a wok and fry the onion, garlic and chillies.
2. Add the tamarind pulp, coconut milk and brown sugar, and let it simmer for a few minutes.
3. Add the peanuts and cook for a few minutes. Blend to form a smooth paste.

Chef's Tip

To get more of an authentic flavour, you can add fish sauce with tamarind pulp, coconut milk and brown sugar. I haven't added it in this recipe since kids don't like its smell much.

Chicken in Red Curry

Serves: 4

Ingredients

To grind

- Coriander seeds – 1 tbsp, roasted
- Cumin seeds – 1 tsp, roasted
- Galangal – 1 small piece
- Garlic – 4–5 cloves
- Dried shrimp paste – ¼ tsp
- Red chillies – 6–8, soaked
- Lemongrass – 1 piece
- Onion – 1

For the curry

- Chicken – 750 gms
- Coconut milk – 400 ml
- Chicken stock – 1 cup
- Oil – 3–4 tbsp
- Salt – to taste
- Fish sauce – 1 tbsp
- Fresh red chillies – 2–3
- Palm sugar – 2 tsp
- Basil leaves – a few

Method

1. Grind all the ingredients mentioned above to a smooth paste.

2. Heat the oil and fry the paste for 2 minutes. Add the coconut milk and simmer.
3. Add the chicken, salt and stock.
4. Add the fish sauce, palm sugar, fresh red chillies and some basil leaves and simmer. Cook till the chicken is tender.
5. Serve with sliced red chillies and flavoured jasmine rice.

Flavoured jasmine rice

Ingredients

- Jasmine rice – 1 cup, washed and soaked for 15 minutes
- Water or stock – 1½ cup
- Lemongrass – 1-inch stalk
- Kaffir lime leaves – 3–4
- Basil leaves – a few, torn
- Veg seasoning – 1 tsp
- Chillies – optional
- Oil – 1½ tbsp

Method

1. Put oil and all the ingredients in the rice cooker and keep on cook mode.
2. Serve with Thai red curry.

Jhatpat Makhanwala

Serves: 2

Ingredients

- Coriander powder – 1 tsp
- Turmeric – a pinch
- Chilli powder – 1 tsp
- Garam masala – 1 tsp
- Salt to taste

To blend

- Onion –1, sautéed a bit in oil
- Red Kashmiri chillies – 2–3
- Cashews – 6
- Tomatoes – 3–4 (alternatively, tomato paste or purée – 100 gms)
- Ginger–garlic and green chilli paste – 2 tsp

Blend to a smooth paste.

For the makhani

Ingredients

- Paneer –150 gms
- Cream – 2 tsp
- Shaan masala or makhanwala masala – 3–4 tsp
- Butter – 2 tbsp
- Bay leaf – 1–2
- Kasuri methi – 1 tbsp

Method

1. Put butter in a pan, add the bay leaf and stir for a second. Next add the ground paste and cook.
2. Add all the dry masalas—coriander powder, turmeric, chilli powder, garam masala, salt—and fry well till the masala cooks and butter releases. Do it for approximately 10–12 minutes. If using a ready makhani masala powder like Shaan, then omit all the masalas and just add 2–3 tsp.
3. Add kasuri methi, water to adjust the gravy and the paneer. Let it simmer for a minute, switch off the gas, finish with cream and serve.

Calorie Count

Cream can be replaced with hung curd/milk and butter can be substituted with olive oil or any other healthy oil.

Missi Roti

Serves: 4

Ingredients

- Besan – 1 cup
- Atta – 1 cup
- Flour – 1 cup
- Spinach – ½ bunch (15–18 leaves), finely chopped
- Green chillies – 2–3, minced
- Salt – to taste
- Red chilli powder – to taste
- Ajwain – a pinch
- Shahi jeera – ½ tsp
- Water – as needed
- Ghee – 3–4 tbsp

Method

1. Mix the flour, atta, besan, salt, ajwain, green chillies, red chilli powder and shahi jeera.
2. Add the spinach and 1 tbsp ghee. Knead into a firm dough using water little by little. Divide the dough into 5 equal parts and roll each into a round ball.
3. Roll out each ball on a floured surface into a round roti, apply ghee on top and cut into a long strip.
4. Stack all the strips one on top of the other and roll like a snail or Swiss roll and flatten it with your fingers.
5. Roll it into a ¼-inch roti. Cook on a tawa on medium flame, applying ghee on either side.

Chicken in Oyster Sauce (p. 116)

Chicken Satay (p. 122)

Cheese and Broccoli Tikki and Spaghetti with Garlic Sauce on a Sizzler Plate (p. 140)

Chicken in Red Curry (p. 124)

Pan-Fried Noodles (p.120)

Manchow Soup (p. 114)

Grilled Chicken in Paprika Sauce with Brown Rice (p. 132)

Baked Enchiladas (p. 129)

Baked Enchiladas

Serves: 8

For the fajita filling

Ingredients

- Olive oil – 1 tbsp
- Onion – 2 slices
- Paneer strips – 400 gms
- Peppers (red, yellow and green) – ½ each, sliced
- Cumin powder – ½ tsp
- Tomato – 2, blanched and chopped
- Red cayenne powder – ½ tsp
- Aromatic seasoning – 1 tsp
- Mexican seasoning – ½ tsp
- Salt – to taste

Method

1. Put oil in a pan and sauté the onions.
2. Add the peppers and stir-fry. Add the tomatoes.
3. Add all the seasonings—salt, cayenne pepper powder, cumin powder, Mexican seasoning and aromatic seasoning.
4. Add the paneer pieces.

For the frijoles refritos

Ingredients

- Dried kidney beans –1 cup, boiled and mashed
- Onion – 2, chopped

- Tomatoes – 3, skinned, deseeded and chopped
- Butter/olive oil – ½ tbsp
- Mexican seasoning – 1 tsp
- Cheddar cheese – 50 gms, grated
- Salt – to taste
- Chilli flakes – ½ tsp

Method

1. Soak the beans for 6–8 hours and boil till tender.
2. Drain and mash it.
3. In a pan, fry the onion in olive oil. Add tomatoes, salt and chilli flakes.
4. Add the mashed beans. Cook until the mixture comes together.
5. Add the cheese and all the seasonings.

If you are using canned beans, there is no need to soak or boil.

For the Mexican rice

Ingredients

- Rice (cooked) – 2 cups
- Mixed vegetables – 100 gms
- Mushrooms – 4–5, diced
- Onion – ½, chopped
- Tomato – 1, chopped
- Mexican seasoning – 2 tsp
- Parsley – to garnish
- Olive oil – 2 tbsp
- Cumin powder – ½ tsp
- Cayenne pepper powder– ½ tsp
- Salt – to taste

Method

1. Heat oil in a pan and stir-fry the onion till translucent.
2. Stir in mushrooms and sauté for a few minutes.
3. Next add all the vegetables.
4. Add the seasoning. Garnish with parsley and use as stuffing in fajitas or tacos.

To assemble

Ingredients

- Tortilla wrap – 8
- Fajita filling – 2 cups
- Mexican rice- 1½ cups
- Frijoles refritos – 1 cup
- Nacho chips – 4–5, crushed
- Cheddar and mozzarella cheese – a handful, grated
- Tomato sauce – 2 ladles
- Butter to apply

Method

1. Warm the tortilla wrap and apply butter.
2. Put a layer of fajita filling.
3. Add refried beans, Mexican rice and crushed chips.
4. Roll and place it on a buttered baking dish.
5. Pour the tomato sauce and the cheese.
6. Bake at 160 degrees for 15–18 minutes or till the cheese melts.

Chef's Tip

Aromatic seasoning is a vegetarian seasoning. Alternatively, you can use any organic seasoning that you prefer.

Grilled Chicken in Paprika Sauce with Brown Rice

Serves: 2

For the marinade

Ingredients

- Chicken leg (boneless) – 250 gms, diced
- Mixed herbs – 1 tsp
- Pepper powder and salt – to taste
- Garlic paste – 1 tbsp
- Olive oil – 1 tbsp
- Balsamic vinegar – a few drops
- Oats – 2 tbsp

Method

1. Marinate the chicken in the above ingredients for 20 minutes and coat it in oats.
2. Sauté or grill the chicken in a pan till done. It should get a nice glaze. Keep aside.

For the paprika sauce

Ingredients

- Onion –1, chopped
- Tomato puree – 1 cup
- Paprika – 5 tsp
- Butter – 4 tbsp
- Fresh cream – 75 ml
- Mushroom – 4–6, sautéed in butter
- Stock – 1 cup

- Parsley – 1 tbsp, chopped
- Flour – 2 tbsp
- Wine – 30 ml(optional)
- Salt and pepper – to taste

Method

1. In a pan, sauté the mushrooms with a little butter and keep aside.
2. Put oil/butter and fry the onion and sprinkle the paprika flakes. Add the flour and cook well.
3. Next, add the chicken, tomato puree and season with salt and pepper.
4. Add wine, some stock and cook for a few minutes. Add the mushrooms, fresh cream and parsley.
5. In a flat dish make a border of herb rice and place the chicken in the centre.
6. Cover with the sauce, add the parsley and serve hot.

Calorie Control

I prefer to use labneh instead of cream as a healthier alternative, and you can't even tell the difference. As mentioned earlier, you can also use jowar or oat flour instead of regular flour.

For the mashed potatoes

Ingredients

- Butter – 1½ tbsp
- Parsley – 10 gms, chopped
- Potatoes – 200 gms, boiled

- Cream – 30 ml
- Salt and pepper – to taste
- Garlic bread seasoning (store-bought) – 1 tsp

Method

1. Boil the potatoes and mash with a potato masher.
2. Melt the butter in a pan and add the potato.
3. Mix well, add salt and pepper. Add garlic bread seasoning at this stage.
4. Lastly, add the cream and mix well. Sprinkle some parsley.

For the spinach brown rice pilaf

Ingredients

- Boiled brown rice – 1 cup
- Spinach puree – 2 tbsp
- Garlic – 1 tbsp, minced
- Olive oil – 2 tbsp
- Salt and pepper – to taste

Method

1. Sauté the garlic in olive oil and add the spinach puree.
2. Next, add the rice and season with salt and pepper and serve.

Chicken Alfredo with Fettuccine

Serves: 2

Ingredients

- Chicken (boneless) – 50 gms, sliced
- Mushroom – 3–4, sliced
- Garlic – ½ tsp, minced
- Butter – 1 tbsp
- Barley atta – 1 tbsp
- Milk – 100 ml
- Fresh cream – 2 tbsp
- Mixed herbs – ¼ tsp
- Fresh parsley – to garnish
- Salt and pepper – to taste
- Fettuccine – 100 gms
- Parmesan cheese – 50 gms, grated

Method

1. Boil the fettuccine pasta in lots of water with salt till al dente (should have a bite).
2. In a pan, heat the butter and fry the garlic. Add the chicken and keep stirring till it turns white. Put in the mushrooms next and stir for a few seconds.
3. Then add the barley flour and stir well till the chicken is coated. Start pouring in the milk gradually.
4. Once mixed, add the remaining milk and let the sauce cook on a slow flame. Season with salt, pepper and mixed herbs.

5. Toss in the fettuccine, coat well, add the cream and check for seasoning. Garnish with fresh parsley, sprinkle some grated Parmesan cheese and serve with garlic bread.

Chef's Tip

I have replaced refined flour with a healthier option, barley atta, in this recipe and, trust me, it adds amazing flavour to the sauce. And the best part is, the children won't know the difference!

Cannelloni Florentine

Serves: 4

For the cannelloni

Ingredients

- Ready to use lasagne sheets (fresh) – 5
- Salt – 1 tsp
- Oil (for cooking the pasta) – 2 tbsp
- Water – for boiling

Method

Boil the pasta for 2–3 minutes and use as required.

For the filling

Ingredients

- Mushrooms – 1 cup, sliced
- Baby corn – 2–3, sliced
- Broccoli – ½ bunch, blanched, drained and finely chopped (optional)
- Green olives – 6–8, sliced
- Zucchini – ½ chopped
- Garlic – 1 tsp, chopped
- Spring onions – 1–2, finely chopped
- Dried oregano – 1 tsp
- Grated processed cheese – ½ cup
- Butter – 1 tbsp
- Salt and black pepper powder – to taste

Method

Sauté all the ingredients (except cheese) in a pan, taking care not to overcook. The veggies should remain nice and crunchy. Switch off the gas and add the cheese.

For the classic arrabbiata

Ingredients

- Tomato pulp – 2 cups
- Garlic – 2 cloves, chopped
- Basil (fresh) – a few leaves
- Chilli flakes – 1 tsp
- Olive oil – 2 tbsp
- Sugar – a pinch
- Salt and pepper – to taste

Method

Heat oil in a pan, add the garlic and tomatoes and cook, seasoning with basil, sugar, salt and pepper and some chilli flakes. Cook for about 15–20 minutes, or till the oil releases on top.

For the spinach sauce

Ingredients

- Spinach puree – ½ cup
- White sauce – 1 cup
- Cream – 4 tbsp
- Garlic – 1 tsp, chopped

- Olive oil/butter – 2 tsp
- Veg seasoning – ½ tsp

Method

1. Sauté the garlic along with the rest of the ingredients (except cheese).
2. Season with salt and pepper and some veg seasoning. Switch off the gas and add cream.

To assemble

1. Butter a baking dish. Put the filling in the cannelloni and roll it like a spring roll. Lay it in the dish. There will be 2–3 rolls.
2. Spread the classic arrabbiata sauce over the rolls.
3. Pour the creamy spinach sauce over and sprinkle cheese and gratinate in a preheated oven for 20–25 minutes at 160–170 degrees, or till it has browned a bit and is completely heated.

Chef's Tip

Veg seasoning, butter and cheese contain excess salt, so please check and add salt.

Calorie Control

You can substitute the ingredients with healthier options of your choice. There will be no difference in appearance.

Cheese and Broccoli Tikki and Spaghetti with Garlic Sauce on a Sizzler Plate

Serves: 2

Ingredients

- Olive oil – 1 tsp
- Onions – ¼ cup, finely chopped
- Ginger–garlic paste – 1 tsp
- Green chillies – 1 tsp, finely chopped
- Broccoli – ½ tsp, finely chopped
- Salt – to taste
- Potatoes – ½ cup, boiled and grated
- Grated mozzarella cheese – 2 tbsp
- Wholewheat breadcrumbs (for coating) – ¼ cup
- Olive oil for cooking – 2 tsp

Method

1. Heat the oil in a non-stick pan; add the onions, ginger–garlic paste and green chillies and sauté for 2 minutes while stirring continuously.
2. Add the broccoli and salt and sauté on a slow flame for another 5–7 minutes or till the broccoli is almost cooked.
3. Remove from the flame, add the potatoes and cheese and mix well. Keep aside to cool.
4. Divide the mixture into 4 equal portions and shape each portion into flat tikkis. Alternatively make tikkis of desired shapes using different moulds as shown in the picture.

5. Roll each tikki in the breadcrumbs and keep aside.
6. Heat a non-stick pan and cook each tikki using minimum oil till it turns golden brown on both sides.

For the garlic sauce

Ingredients

- Garlic – 2 tbsp, minced
- Tomato puree – ½ cup
- Tomato ketchup – 2–3 tbsp
- Salt and white pepper powder – to taste
- Stock – ¾ cup
- Cornflour paste – 1 tbsp
- Oil – 1 tbsp

Method

1. Heat the oil and add the minced garlic. Fry for a few seconds.
2. Add the tomato puree and cook for 5 minutes.
3. Add the salt and white pepper powder.
4. Add the tomato ketchup and the stock.
5. Add the cornflour paste. Cook for a minute and use.

To assemble

- Broccoli tikki – 2 tikkis
- Spaghetti boiled – 1 cup
- Cabbage – 2–3 leaves
- Grated cheese or cheese slices – ½ cup or 1
- Garlic sauce – 1 cup

- Veggies (blanched carrot, baby corn, spinach, sautéed mushroom, onions) and French fries – ½ cup

Method

1. Heat the sizzler plate very well.
2. Place cabbage leaves on the plate.
3. Place spaghetti in the centre, top it with tikkis.
4. Place veggies around the spaghetti.
5. Pour the garlic sauce over the top.
6. Place the cheese slice over the cutlet and let it sizzle and gratinate.

4

Party Planning

PARTY PLANNING CAN be a tedious task if not done right. And the most difficult part is the food. If your own kids are picky eaters, imagine a whole bunch of them! What would you feed them?

The main thing about party food is that it needs to be as easy to eat as possible, like snacks and small meals. No kid likes to sit down and eat a proper dinner at a get-together. There is so much going on—games, dancing, excitedly screaming kids—that it may not be possible for you to personally attend to every individual at all times. What you can ensure is that there are snacks and yummy bites for everyone to dig into.

The following recipes are going to be your go-to guide, not just for kids' parties but also parties with your friends. They are foolproof and simple, yet delicious. It's almost like fast food but not as unhealthy. Enjoy!

Ice Cream Cake Pops

Serves: 8

Ingredients

- Ice cream cones – 8–10
- Cake (crumbled) – 4–6 cups
- Icing/frosting – 1 cup
- Melted milk chocolate – 1 cup
- Melted chocolate (white/pink) – ½ cup
- Gems or candies – as required

Method

1. Cut the ice cream cones a little from the top to make them smaller.
2. Mix the icing into the crumbled cake and shape into round balls.
3. Insert a stick into each cake pop and refrigerate.
4. Dip the cold cake pop in melted chocolate, tap off any excess and place it on the ice cream cone.
5. Drizzle some pink or white chocolate on one half of the cake pop.
6. Pour sprinkles and place Gems on top and let it set.

For the frosting

Ingredients

- Butter – 50 gms
- Icing sugar – 100 gms

Ice Cream Cake Pops (p. 144)

Mini Burgers (p. 147)

Chocolate Mini Tarts (p. 152)

Muffin Pizza (p. 154)

Banana Boston Cream Shot (p. 150)

Fruit Jelly Boats (p. 155)

Chocolate Fondue (p. 158)

Watermelon Cranberry Mocktail (p. 149)

Method

1. Use an electric beater to blend the butter and icing sugar till smooth and fluffy. Use as desired.

Caterpillar Sandwiches

Serves: 2

Ingredients

- Brown bread slices – 16, cut into roundels
- Butter – to spread
- Cream cheese – to spread
- Nutella – to spread
- Apple – 1, sliced into roundels
- Banana – 1, sliced into roundels

Method

1. Butter the bread roundels and spread Nutella on one half and cream cheese on the other half.
2. With the cream cheese pair an apple or strawberry.
3. With the Nutella put a slice of banana and make the roundel into sandwiches and keep aside.

To assemble

1. On a large platter place the sandwiches in an S shape in the form of a caterpillar.
2. Add a tomato for the head with some details of eyes and antennae as shown in the picture.

Chef's Tip

I would substitute apple with strawberries when in season.

Mini Burgers

Serves: 10

For the chicken cutlets

Ingredients

- Chicken – 200 gms, minced
- Onion –1½ tbsp
- Ginger, garlic – 2 tsp, minced
- Egg – ½
- Breadcrumbs – 2 tbsp
- Salt – to taste
- Red chilli powder – ½ tsp
- Worcestershire sauce – 1 tsp
- Coriander leaves – 1 tsp
- Green chillies (optional, if you like it spicy)
- Pepper powder – ½ tsp
- Mozzarella cheese – cut into squares
- Oil – 2–3 tbsp, for frying

Method

1. Mix all the above-mentioned ingredients (except cheese) in a bowl and keep in the fridge for 30 minutes.
2. Make small rounds of the mixture, like a tikki, and stuff mozzarella cheese in the centre. After that, fry them in oil till done on both sides and golden in colour.

For the coleslaw

Ingredients

- Carrot – 1, grated
- Cabbage – 2 tbsp, grated
- Mayonnaise – 3 tbsp

Method

1. Mix all the ingredients together to make coleslaw.

To assemble

- Buns – 6
- Butter – to apply
- Lettuce – 10 (1 for each)
- Tomato ketchup – 5 tbsp
- Chilli sauce – 2 tbsp
- Onion – 10 rings (1 for each)
- Cheese slices – 5 (½ slice for each)
- Toothpicks – a few

Method

1. Butter the buns. Place lettuce, a cutlet, sliced onion, a dollop of tomato ketchup, chilli sauce and a slice of cheese on a buttered slice of the bun.
2. Cover with another slice and secure with a toothpick.
3. Serve with chips and coleslaw on the side.

Calorie Control

The chicken cutlets can be air-fried with just a spray of oil.

Watermelon Cranberry Mocktail

Serves: 2

Ingredients

- Cranberry juice – 1 glass
- Sprite – 250 ml
- Watermelon juice – 1 glass
- Lemon – 1 for garnish
- Watermelon cubes – for garnish
- Mint leaves – for garnish

Method

1. Mix the cranberry juice, Sprite and watermelon juice in a big bowl and serve with some mint leaves and watermelon cubes in glasses. Slice the lemon for garnishing.

FANCY DESSERT GLASSES

Banana Boston Cream Shot

For the banana cake

Ingredients

- Bananas – 2, mashed
- Butter – 100 gms
- Flour – 100 gms
- Castor sugar –100 gms
- Eggs – 2
- Baking powder – ¼ tsp
- Vanilla essence – 1 tsp
- Milk – 50 ml
- Baking loaf tin – 7-inch

Method

1. Beat the butter and castor sugar till light and creamy. Add the eggs, one at a time.
2. Fold in the flour along with the baking powder and add a dash of vanilla essence.
3. Add the mashed bananas. Do not over mix.
4. Add milk.
5. Pour the batter into a 7-inch loaf tin and bake it in a preheated oven at 170 degrees for 20–25 minutes or until a toothpick inserted in the centre comes out clean.

For the Boston cream

Ingredients

- Cooked or readymade custard – 1 cup
- Whipped cream – 1 cup

Method

1. Mix the custard and whipped cream and keep aside.

For the chocolate sauce

Ingredients

- Fresh cream – 200 ml
- Dark chocolate – 400 gms

Method

1. Heat the cream and add the chocolate. Whisk till the chocolate melts.

To assemble

1. Take fancy shot glasses and add a layer of the banana cake after crumbling it.
2. Pipe a layer of banana Boston cream.
3. Pipe a layer of chocolate sauce, top with another layer of cream and a final sprinkling of cake.

Chef's Tip

Add some Oreo crumbs or brownie bits.

Chocolate Mini Tarts

Serves: 8–10

For the pastry

Ingredients

- Flour – 200 gms
- Icing sugar – 40 gms
- Butter – 100 gms
- Chilled water – 30–40 ml
- Egg – 1

Method

1. In a bowl, mix the flour and icing sugar.
2. Add butter with your fingertips until the mixture resembles breadcrumbs.
3. Add water until it sticks together as dough.
4. Form it into a ball, wrap in cling film and chill for half an hour.
5. Roll out the pastry and line small tart moulds. Prick with a fork.
6. Chill in the fridge for 25 minutes.
7. Blind bake in the oven for 15–18 minutes at 160 degrees.
8. Remove and use an egg wash to act as a coating and again bake for 5 minutes.

For the filling

Ingredients

- Chocolate – 200 gms
- Cream – 100 gms
- Butter – 5 gms

Method

1. Heat the chocolate and cream together on a double boiler till the chocolate melts.
2. Add the butter, whisk, and keep aside to cool.
3. Put it in a piping bag with a star nozzle.
4. Pipe it in the cooled tart shells and add some sprinkles on top. Serve.

Muffin Pizza

Serves: 10

Ingredients

- Tomato – 5–6 big, chopped
- Garlic – 2 tbsp, minced
- Onion – 1 big, chopped
- Tomato ketchup – 2–3 tbsp
- Olive oil/ butter – 3 tbsp
- Salt – to taste
- Chilli flakes – to taste (optional)
- Mixed herbs
- English muffins – 10
- Mozzarella cheese – 150 gms, grated

Method

1. Put oil in a pan and fry the garlic and onion for 2 minutes.
2. Add the chopped tomato, tomato ketchup, salt, chilli flakes, mixed herbs and cook till the oil separates.
3. Let the sauce cool and run it through a blender.
4. Cut the English savoury muffins into half.
5. Spread the tomato sauce on the muffins and sprinkle the mozzarella cheese and some herbs. Bake for about 5–10 minutes in the oven at 160 degrees or until the cheese has melted.

Fruit Jelly Boats

Serves: 6

Ingredients

- Oranges – 8–10
- Kiwi juice – 400 ml
- Blood orange syrup – 100 ml
- Blue cotton candy syrup – 100 ml
- Gelatin – 30 gms for each jelly
- Toothpicks – a few

Method

1. Slice the oranges in half and scoop out the flesh.
2. Take 30 gms gelatin, add a little water and heat in the microwave till transparent. Let it cool a bit and add to the kiwi juice.
3. Since the blood orange and blue cotton candy are syrups, dilute 100 ml of each with 300 ml of water and add gelatin in the same way.
4. Place the orange halves in a muffin tin and fill each with blood orange, kiwi or cotton candy. Refrigerate until set.
5. Make sails with rectangles of heavy paper and stick them on toothpicks to form a mast.
6. When the jelly has set, slice oranges in half again to make quarters and plant the paper sails into each quarter.
7. Place boats on the 'sea' and serve to your delighted kids at the party.

Chef's Tip

Alternatively you can use fresh strawberry and kiwi purees. Cook them with sugar and set with gelatin. You can then use it as mentioned above for a fresher, home-made experience.

Caramel Marshmallow Popcorn

Serves: 4

Ingredients

- Plain ACT II popcorn – 1 packet
- White marshmallows – 1 small packet
- Butter – 2–3 tbsp
- Brown sugar – 2–3 tbsp

Method

1. Follow the packet instructions to make the popcorn in the microwave. Once ready, keep aside.
2. Take some butter in a pan and add brown sugar to it. As it starts to caramelize, pour in a handful of marshmallows and take it off the heat.
3. Coat the popcorn with the mixture properly and serve your quick and yummy caramel marshmallow popcorn to the kids on movie night.

Chocolate Fondue

Serves: 4

Ingredients

- Dark chocolate – 100 gms
- Semi-sweet chocolate – 100 gms
- Cream – 100 ml

Method

1. Chop the chocolates and keep aside.
2. In a pan, put the cream and bring it to a boil.
3. Add the chocolate and take it off the flame.
4. Whisk the chocolate until smooth.
5. Pour it into the chocolate fondue pot.
6. Serve with bananas, sliced pound cake and marshmallows.

Chef's Tip

I always treat the kids to strawberries and Oreo cookies along with this which they love to indulge in, guilt-free.

5

Cooking Together

COOKING WITH YOUR child is absolutely great. It helps you spend time with your little one, giving you a mini helper in the kitchen at the same time! So why not do it?

Jokes apart, I've mentioned before how cooking together could be a very good way to bond with your kids. It can be super fun and all you have to do is know how to make it interactive.

I have a few amazing recipes lined up which you could involve your little ones in and, believe me, they'll want to do this more often!

Piggy Buns

Serves: 4

Ingredients

- Flour – 125 gms
- Yeast – 10 gms
- Salt – 5 gms
- Butter – 7 gms
- Sugar – 5 gms
- Water – 75–90 ml
- Milk/egg for brushing
- Some cloves or chocolate chips for face details

Method

1. Dissolve yeast and sugar in 2 tsp water and leave it aside.
2. Make a well in the flour and add the yeast in the centre.
3. Add water to make soft dough.
4. Cream the butter and salt, and knead it into the dough.
5. Cover with a muslin cloth and keep in a warm place to double.
6. After 15–18 minutes knock down the dough. Roll it to a thickness of .5 cm.

Piggy Buns (p. 160)

Ferrolicious Cupcake (p. 164)

Quinoa, Corn and Mushroom-Stuffed Baked Potatoes (p. 177)

Canapés (p. 171)

Cheese Biscuits (p. 170)

Cut-Out Vanilla Cookies (p. 168)

Paneer Shashlik with BBQ Sauce (p. 172)

Nachos and Salsa (p.162)

For the piggy buns

Cut shapes from the dough with cookie cutters as given below.

- 1 oval shape for the face
- 2 small triangles for the ears
- 1 tiny circle for the nose
- 2 chocolate chips for the eyes

1. Place the oval-shaped dough on the baking tray.
2. Brush with a little milk and place the triangle shapes to form ears.
3. Place the little circle on the centre to form the nose.
4. Place the chocolate chips to form eyes.
5. Brush with milk or egg.
6. Bake at 180 degrees for 20 minutes.

Nachos and Salsa

Serves: 4

Ingredients

- Nachos chips – 10
- Shredded cheddar cheese – ½ cup
- Milk – 2–3 tbsp
- Jalapeño – 4, chopped

Method

1. Place the nachos on a serving dish. Melt the cheese, add the milk and whisk until creamy.
2. Pour the mixture over the nachos. Sprinkle the chopped jalapeño.

Chef's Tip

Use the mild cheddar, yellow in colour, for the picky eaters to get excited and feel like the dish is straight from a restaurant. I mix a bit of Britannia cheese as well for better balance of taste.

Calorie Control

I've used milk in this recipe instead of cream to make it a lighter cheese sauce.

For the salsa

Ingredients

- Onion – 2, chopped
- Garlic – 3 cloves, chopped
- Olive oil – 2 tbsp
- Salt – to taste
- Mexican seasoning – 1tsp
- Green chilli – 4, chopped
- Parsley (fresh) – 1 tsp, chopped
- Tomatoes – 4, blanched, peeled, deseeded and chopped
- Lime juice – 2 tbsp
- Tomato paste – 1 tsp
- Tomato juice – 3 tbsp
- Jalapeño – 2–3, chopped

Method

1. Put oil in a pan, fry the garlic and onion till translucent.
2. Remove in a bowl. Add the chopped tomato, tomato paste, green chillies and jalapeño.
3. Mix well and add the lime juice, tomato juice, salt and Mexican seasoning.
4. Add the fresh parsley and serve.

Ferrolicious Cupcake

Serves: 10

Ingredients

- Flour – 100 gms
- Sugar – 100 gms
- Butter – 100 gms
- Baking powder – ¼ tsp
- Milk – 50 ml
- Vanilla extract – ½ tsp
- Cocoa powder – 1½ tbsp
- Chocolate chips – 150 gms
- Eggs – 2

Method

1. In a bowl, mix flour, baking powder and cocoa powder and keep aside.
2. In another bowl, cream the butter and sugar with a beater till light and pale.
3. Add the eggs, one at a time, to the butter–sugar batter and keep beating at a low speed. Add the vanilla extract.
4. Next add the flour, cocoa powder and baking powder mixture to this.
5. Add the chocolate chips and mix everything together by pouring milk and blending gently with a spatula. Do not over mix.
6. Take a muffin tray and line with cupcake liners. Fill ¾ with the batter.

7. Bake at 160–170 degrees for 20–25 minutes.
8. Insert a toothpick in the centre of the muffin to check if it's done. If it comes out clean, it is.

For the ganache and toppings

Ingredients

- Chocolate – 100 gms
- Cream – 50 ml
- Nutella – 2 tbsp
- Ferrero Rocher – 10

Method

1. Melt the chocolate and cream on a double boiler.
2. Whisk together to combine and add the Nutella.
3. Put this luscious, mouth-watering frosting in a piping bag with a star nozzle.
4. With the help of the piping bag swirl some frosting over the cooled cupcakes and top each one with a Ferrero Rocher chocolate.

Chef's Tip

You can substitute the Ferrero Rocher with KitKat or Snickers. Both children and adults love digging into these heavenly cupcakes.

Please refer to pictures for filling the piping bags and icing and decorating your cupcakes.

Red Velvet Cupcake

Serves: 8–10

For the cupcake

Ingredients

- Flour — 60 gms
- Wheat flour – 60 gms
- Castor sugar – 125 gms
- Butter – 50 gms
- Cocoa powder –15 gms
- Vanilla extract – 1 tsp
- Baking powder – 1 tsp
- Baking soda – ¼ tsp
- Egg – 1
- Beetroot juice – 3 tbsp
- Buttermilk – 85 ml
- Vinegar – 2–3 drops

Method

1. In a bowl, mix the flour, wheat flour, cocoa powder, baking powder and baking soda.
2. In another bowl, cream the butter and sugar till pale.
3. Add the egg to the butter and sugar and beat well. Add the flour mixture to this.
4. Finally add the beetroot juice to the buttermilk and vinegar and pour into the batter.
5. Divide the batter into 6 portions for the cupcakes.
6. Bake in an oven for 15–20 minutes at 160 degrees.

7. Then use the cream cheese icing on your red velvet cupcakes and decorate them with hearts and other cute sprinkles.

For the cream cheese icing

Ingredients

- Butter – 100 gms
- Icing sugar – 200 gms
- Cream cheese – 50 gms

Method

1. Beat the butter in a bowl and add the icing sugar until stiff.
2. Add the cream cheese. Put it in a piping bag.
3. Pipe on the cooled cupcakes.

Cut-Out Vanilla Cookies

Serves: 15

Ingredients

- Butter – 90 gms
- Sugar – 100 gms
- Milk – 30 ml/1egg
- Vanilla extract – ½ tsp
- Flour – 1½ cup
- Baking powder – ½ tsp

Method

1. In a bowl, mix flour and baking powder and keep aside.
2. Cream the butter and sugar until light and pale.
3. Add the milk/egg and vanilla extract to the butter and sugar. To this add the flour mixture.
4. Mix gently, and if you think the dough is too sticky, add a little flour. But do it sparingly as too much flour will make the dough tough.
5. Place the dough in a plastic bag and let it rest in the refrigerator for 1 hour.
6. Sprinkle flour on a surface and place the dough on it.
7. Then roll it out to a thickness of about ¼ inch.
8. Cut into shapes after having dipped the cutter in the flour.
9. Place the cookies on a greased tray.
10. Bake at 160 degrees for 20 minutes, till the sides are slightly browned.

They will be soft in the centre but will set once they cool.

For the sugar icing

Ingredients

- Boiled water – 2–3 tbsp
- Icing sugar (sifted) – 100 gms
- Food colour – a few drops

Method

1. Divide the icing sugar into 2–3 bowls, add 1 tsp boiled water in each and mix well.
2. Add food colour of your choice in the icing sugar to make a thick paste and spread on the cookies.
3. Decorate with some sprinkles, Gems and mixed sugar strands.

Cheese Biscuits

Serves: 4

Ingredients

- Flour – 120 gms
- Cheese (grated) – 80 gms
- Butter – 75 gms
- Baking powder – ½ tsp
- Salt – ½ tsp
- Mustard powder – ¼ tsp
- Chilli powder – ½ tsp
- Fresh cream – 3 tbsp
- Poppy seeds – a little
- Egg – ½ or 1 tbsp milk

Method

1. Mix flour, salt, baking powder, mustard powder, and chilli powder in a bowl.
2. In another bowl cream the butter and cheese till smooth.
3. Add the fresh cream to this butter–cheese mixture.
4. Fold in the flour mixture.
5. Knead to make a smooth dough.
6. Cling wrap the dough and refrigerate for 15 minutes.
7. Roll it out to ¼-inch thickness and cut shapes using a biscuit cutter.
8. Place on a lightly greased tray. Brush with egg wash or milk.
9. Sprinkle some poppy seeds and bake at 160 degrees for 20–25 minutes, until they turn golden brown.

Canapés

Serves: 4

Ingredients

- White sauce – 3 tbsp
- Mushroom – 3–4, minced
- Mixed herbs – for sprinkling
- Garlic – 1 tbsp, chopped
- Salt and pepper – to taste
- Butter – 2 tsp
- Chilli garlic sauce – 1 tbsp
- Cheese – 3 tbsp, grated
- Canapés/Monaco biscuits – 15–20
- Parsley – a few leaves for garnishing

Method

1. Sauté the mushroom in butter with garlic for 1 minute and season with salt, pepper and mixed herbs.
2. Mix the mushrooms with the white sauce which, ideally, should not be too thick or too thin.
3. Put a spoonful of the mixture on the canapés or Monaco biscuits or crackers.
4. Sprinkle grated cheese, a dot of chilli garlic sauce and garnish with a parsley leaf.

Paneer Shashlik with BBQ Sauce

Serves: 6

For the paneer shashlik

Ingredients

- Paneer –150 gms, cubed
- Salt and pepper – to taste
- Toothpicks – a few
- Olive oil – 1 tbsp

For the BBQ Sauce

Ingredients

- Mustard paste – ¼ tsp
- Balsamic vinegar – ¼ tsp
- Tomato ketchup – 1tsp
- Chilli sauce – ½ tsp
- Garlic paste – ½ tsp
- Chilli flakes – ½ tsp
- Mixed herbs – 1tsp

Method

1. Put the paneer on toothpicks and season with salt and pepper.
2. Mix all the ingredients for BBQ sauce in a bowl and marinate the paneer in it.
3. Heat a pan and fry the paneer with olive oil or butter for a few minutes on each side and serve.

Cheats' Healthy Cupcake

Serves: 6

Ingredients

- Avocado – 1
- Almond flour – 1 cup
- Milk or almond milk – ¼ cup
- Egg –1
- Coco powder – Reduce 1 tsp from ¼ th cup
- Brown sugar – 62.5 gms
- Vanilla extract – ½ tsp
- Baking powder – ¼ tsp
- Baking soda – ¼ tsp
- Coconut milk – 1 tbsp
- Chocolate chips – 25 gms

Method

1. In a bowl, mix the almond flour, cocoa powder, baking powder and baking soda and keep aside.
2. Mash the avocado and beat it with the brown sugar.
3. Add the egg and vanilla extract and mix well.
4. Add the almond flour mixture to the avocado mash and fold it with the almond milk. Add coconut milk to achieve the right consistency.
5. Add the chocolate chips and mix well.
6. Pour this batter in the cupcake liners and bake at 160–170 degrees in a convection oven for 15–20 minutes until you insert a toothpick into the cupcake and it comes out clean. That is when you know your cupcake is well done.

Chef's Tip

The avocado fat replaces the butter or oil in this recipe, and a good-quality cocoa powder really enhances the flavour so our picky eaters will never know what they are consuming!

If you don't have coconut milk, you can add almond milk.

If using store-bought almond flour, then sieve and use the finer version. If not, then blend it into a fine powder, ensuring that the oil does not release.

Fudge Brownie Sundae

Serves: 4

For the brownie (9 pieces)

Ingredients

- Butter – 82.5 gms
- Dark chocolate –100 gms
- Eggs – 1½
- Egg yolk – 1
- Brown sugar – 165 gms
- Vanilla extract– ½ tsp
- Flour – 2 tbsp
- Cocoa powder – 1tbsp

Method

1. Mix the flour and cocoa powder in a bowl and keep aside.
2. Melt the butter and chocolate on a double boiler and keep aside.
3. Beat the egg, egg yolk, vanilla extract and brown sugar till light and fluffy.
4. Add the butter and chocolate mixture to the egg and sugar.
5. Fold in the flour and mix it in the motion of creating the figure 8.
6. Pour the batter in an 8-inch ring mould lined with foil and bake at 180 degrees for 20–25 minutes.

For the chocolate fudge

Ingredients

- Chocolate – 100 gms, melted
- Cream – 50 ml
- Milkmaid – 50 ml

Method

1. Mix the cream and Milkmaid in the cooled, melted chocolate to get amazing chocolate fudge.

To assemble

- Vanilla ice cream – 4 scoops
- Assorted nuts – a handful
- Chocolate fudge
- Chocolate brownie
- Strawberries – a handful
- Whipped cream – 1 spray can

Method

1. Break the brownie into tiny pieces in a bowl and microwave for 10–15 seconds.
2. Cut a handful of strawberries and put on top of the brownie pieces.
3. Scoop the vanilla ice cream on top. Then heat up the chocolate fudge and pour on top of the ice cream.
4. Top with some whipped cream and nuts and let your children indulge.

Quinoa Corn and Mushroom-Stuffed Baked Potatoes

Serves: 6

For the baked potatoes base

Ingredients

- Potatoes – 4, parboiled
- Oil – for brushing
- Salt – to taste

Method

1. Brush the potato with oil and sprinkle a little salt over it.
2. Wrap in an aluminium foil and bake in a preheated oven for 15–18 minutes at a temperature of 160–180 degrees.
3. Cool slightly and cut each baked potato in half.
4. Scoop the centre to make a hole. Keep aside.

For the white sauce

Ingredients

- Butter – 2 tbsp
- Barley atta – 2 tbsp
- Milk – 150 ml
- Stock – 100 ml
- Salt and pepper – to taste

Method

1. Cook the barley atta and butter in a pan with a whisk for 1–2 minutes.
2. Pour in the milk and stock gradually till the sauce thickens but still has a pouring consistency.
3. Cook for a few minutes and season with salt and pepper.

For the filling

Ingredients

- White sauce – 3 tbsp
- Corn –50 gms, boiled
- Mushroom – 3–4, minced
- Quinoa – ¼ cup
- Mozzarella cheese (grated) – 50 gms
- Veg seasoning – ½ tsp
- Spinach – a few leaves, chopped
- Mixed herbs – ½ tsp

Method

1. Mix the white sauce, mushroom, corn, quinoa, chopped spinach, aromatic seasoning and mixed herbs.
2. Put it in a piping bag and pipe into the scooped potatoes.
3. Add the cheese and bake in an oven for 10 minutes at 160 degrees.

For the quinoa

Ingredients

- Quinoa – ¼ cup
- Stock – ¾ cup (Refer to the stock recipe)
- Salt – a pinch

Method

1. Boil the quinoa with the stock and add a pinch of salt till fluffed up. This should take about 15–20 minutes on a low flame.

Acknowledgements

THERE ARE SO many people who have influenced me, touched me in many ways and continue to do so.

To my husband—my friend, my soulmate, my confidant—who is and will always be my biggest support. You always envisioned my path for me, even when I doubted myself. You taught me to always be positive even when I didn't see hope. Thank you for being my teacher and walking beside me on my culinary journey.

To Anita, my teacher and partner in my first venture in the culinary world. You influenced me and helped me discover the hidden teacher in myself.

To my firstborn, Aneeshaa. Although you are just eighteen, had you not pushed me into restarting work, I would've been in a different space today. You not only acted and helped me as a friend, you even played the multiple roles of an assistant, coordinator and research partner. I would not have been able to complete this book without you, my darling Annie. I love you 22 (you know what this means).

To my young and handsome son, Akhil Vaswani. You are one of the inspirations behind this book. Thank you for pushing me to find myself through my work. There have been times when I could not be around because of my work, but you make me proud with the way you have grown into a great human being. I love how you trick me into making something for you. Thank you again for all those amazing moments.

And finally, to my mother, my family and all my well-wishers who have always supported me.

A Note on the Author

Celebrity chef Rakhee Vaswani is a cookery expert and a Cordon Bleu–trained chef who is successfully leading Palate Culinary Studio, a first-of-its-kind initiative equipped with a state-of-the-art kitchen. Her celebrity students include Malaika Arora Khan, Mini Mathur, Radhika and Shaan, Gauri Tejwani, Manasi Joshi Roy and Rakshanda Khan. She writes an online column for I-Diva and has also been featured in various newspapers, magazines and TV shows (including *The Foodie* on Times Now hosted by Kunal Vijaykar and *The Khan Sisters* on Bindass). She is currently hosting her own TV show 'Rewind With Rakhee' on Living Foodz, India's first Foodtainment channel.

She is passionate about her food and believes that it's the perfect remedy for all problems. She also believes strongly in sharing the art of cooking. She uses the best quality ingredients to replicate international cuisines at home with ease. She feels at peace and is happiest when in a kitchen.

This is her first book.

www.palateculinarystudio.com/cooking-studio.php

With Malaika Arora Khan at the launch of Palate Culinary Studio

Malaika trying her hand at cooking

Radhika and Shaan at the launch of my culinary studio

With Raymond Blanc,
one of UK's most celebrated chefs

With French pâtissier and
celebrity chef Eric Lanlard

Healthy Bars

Food scenery

Doing what I love best